The History of
STILTON CHEESE

Drink a pot of ale, eat a scoop of Stilton, every day, you will make 'old bones'.

Nineteenth-century saying, Wymondham.

Stilton, the king of English cheeses, is still served in the bar of The Bell Inn at Stilton as it was in the days of Cooper Thornhill, who worked from this famous hostelry from 1730 to 1759. Thornhill was the east of England agent for the London bankers, Coutts & Co. He was a pioneering businessman who made Stilton a household name throughout the British Isles, eventually bringing this unique cheese to the attention of connoisseurs the world over. Since 1985 The Bell Inn, now a hotel, has been run by Liam McGivern, who serves only the finest Stilton and the very best beer to guests from far and wide.

The History of
STILTON CHEESE

TREVOR HICKMAN

SUTTON PUBLISHING

Sutton Publishing
Phoenix Mill · Thrupp · Stroud
Gloucestershire · GL5 2BU

First published 1995
Reprinted with corrections 1996, 1998, 2001
This edition 2005

Copyright © Trevor Hickman, 1995

ISBN 0–7509–4416–1

British Library Cataloguing in Publication Data
A catalogue record for this book is available from
the British Library.

Typeset in 10/12.5 Photina.
Typesetting and origination by
Sutton Publishing.
Printed and bound in England by
J.H. Haynes & Co. Ltd, Sparkford.

Cover photograph: Stilton cheeses being sold at
Leicester, 1903. (*Reproduced by kind permission of
Leicestershire Museums, Arts and Records Service.*)

The name Stilton and the device
are certification trade marks
vested in the Stilton Cheese
Makers' Association. This is to
ensure that Stilton cheeses are
made only in the designated area
of the UK, to the traditional
recipe.

By the same author:

Around Melton Mowbray in Old Photographs	*Melton Mowbray to Oakham*
Melton Mowbray in Old Photographs	*Leicestershire Memories*
The Vale of Belvoir in Old Photographs	*The Best of East Leicestershire & Rutland*
Around Rutland in Old Photographs	*The Best of Leicestershire*
East of Leicester in Old Photographs	*The Best of Leicester*
The Melton Mowbray Album	*Battlefields of Leicestershire*
The History of the Melton Mowbray Pork Pie	*Market Towns of Leicestershire & Rutland*

The author of *The History
of Stilton Cheese* presenting
a specially bound copy of
the first edition to the
Prime Minister, at The Bell
Inn, Stilton on 3 November
1995. Left to right: Steve
Peace of J.M. Nuttall,
Hartington Creamery; the
author, Trevor Hickman;
Norma Major; Liam
McGivern, landlord of the
Bell Inn; the Prime
Minister, the Right
Honourable John Major,
MP. Photograph by Chris
Lowndes of Peterborough.

CONTENTS

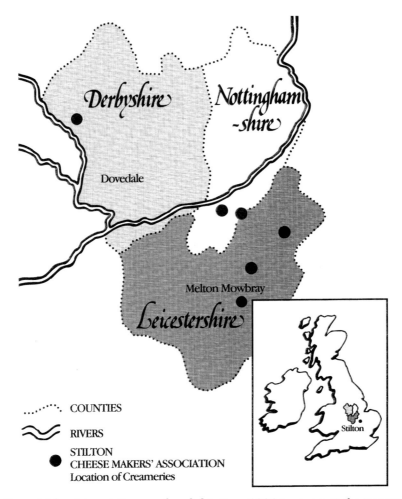

COUNTIES

RIVERS

STILTON
CHEESE MAKERS' ASSOCIATION
Location of Creameries

The Stilton Cheese Makers' Association was founded in June 1936 to represent the interests of its members and to promote the benefits of Stilton cheese. The association also manages the certification trade mark, which protects the name Stilton and authorizes its use only on cheese of the required quality, made in the three counties. Today there are six member companies operating in the region detailed on this plan.

HARTINGTON
J.M. Nuttall, Hartington Creamery, Hartington, Buxton, Derbyshire SK17 0AH

MELTON MOWBRAY
Tuxford & Tebbutt, Thorpe End, Melton Mowbray, Leicestershire LE14 1RE

LONG CLAWSON
Long Clawson Dairy Ltd, Long Clawson, Melton Mowbray, Leicestershire LE14 4PJ

COLSTON BASSETT
Colston Bassett & District Dairy Co. Ltd, Harby Lane, Colston Bassett, Nottingham NG12 3FN

CROPWELL BISHOP
Cropwell Bishop Creamery, Nottingham Road, Cropwell Bishop, Nottingham NG12 3BQ

QUENBY STILTON
Quenby Hall, Near Hungerton, Leicestershire LE7 9JF

INTRODUCTION

Having lived in Wymondham in east Leicestershire for more than sixty years, I have been brought up with the tradition that the Old Manor House in this village is the home of Stilton cheese. Local history has always interested me and for more than thirty years I have endeavoured to piece together the legend that is Stilton cheese. At what point in time was a blue-veined cream cheese developed that could be recognized as Stilton cheese, and above all where was it developed?

All the evidence points to a cream cheese being made in the parish of Wymondham soon after it came under the domination of the Norman settlers in the twelfth century. However, a cheese of this type would not be exclusive to any district in England. The first cheese made in any quantity at this period was probably a seasonal cheese made from ewes' milk. Stilton, of course, is made from cows' milk. When did this form of cheese arrive in the small town of Stilton? Who made the first blue-veined cream cheese from cows' milk in the district around Melton Mowbray? There is no way of answering these questions. Many individuals living in farming communities in this area would make cheese from their surplus milk. When it was offered for sale, it would have been given a variety of names. However, a blue-veined cream cheese made from cows' milk was produced by farmers at Wymondham as soon as pastures were enclosed within the open-field system. Possibly the monks of Kirby Bellars Priory also made a blue-veined cream cheese from cows' milk, commencing in the fourteenth century.

Undoubtedly the cheese we now recognize as Stilton was developed because of increased demand, most probably as a result of the development of road links throughout the country following the road-reforming decrees of the reign of Charles II and the toll-road acts of the eighteenth century. The most important highway to be developed was the Great North Road, on which the town of Stilton had been a stopping point for centuries, supporting many generations of travellers on their journeys. Cheese as a food had long been available in this small town. With the development of the coaching trade, not only was cheese carried on journeys to be eaten as required, but it was also purchased for retail and consumption in the towns and cities that were the eventual destinations of the travellers. So 'the cheese of Stilton' was developed.

No doubt a blue-veined cream cheese had been on offer with many other types of cheese in the various hostelries in the town. Some would have been made locally from ewes' milk. Stilton cheese, however, is unique; it has its own distinctive taste and quality when it has reached maturity. Initially, this type of cheese would have been produced in all shapes and sizes, not unlike some of the European and Mediterranean varieties still available today. Some form of standard was required because of the quantities necessary to maintain the supply. It is possible that these standards were introduced by Mrs Frances Pawlett of Wymondham, a cheese-maker of high repute working in the early years of the eighteenth century. Although eighteenth-century researchers, who possibly questioned her on the subject, credit her with being the 'inventor' of this cheese, Mrs Pawlett did not introduce a blue-veined cream cheese to Stilton; rather she applied the standards of the day, rationalizing shape, size and quality.

Mrs Pawlett and her husband would have been the leading force in the eighteenth century, supplying the town of Stilton with cheese. Of course, they would not have had exclusive rights to the market. Many other wholesalers from Rutland and Leicestershire would have supplied cheese, connecting the many cheese-making dairies with this lucrative outlet. Quality and quantity were both required, a goal no single dairy could achieve. Mrs Pawlett set a standard, producing her own cheese and acting as the 'middleman', and selected only the best of other dairies' cheese for delivery to Stilton. She would have had her competitors.

The town of Stilton was one of the most important terminuses on the Great North Road, located approximately seventy miles from London, a comfortable day's journey by coach. At its height as a stage coach station, this town was the market-place for retailing vast quantities of Stilton cheeses – thousands would be sold every week. Delivered by the wagon-load, they were stacked high on both sides of the wide main street. The Bell, The Angel, The Talbot and The Woolpack vied with each other for business, offering what they considered to be the best cheeses. Legend has it that Cooper Thornhill, the owner of The Bell, in association with Frances Pawlett, sold the best cheeses in the middle years of the eighteenth century, and his was certainly the first hostelry to offer them. Until Cooper Thornhill became involved, it was also very much a seasonal trade, Stilton cheese only being on offer when available. Later, at the height of the cheese trade during the first half of the nineteenth century, The Angel attained prominence as the leading hostelry in the town. With the arrival of the railways in the 1840s, however, the coaching and posting business collapsed, and with it the cheese market at Stilton, almost overnight.

Woodcut from *Schweizer Chronik* by J. Stumf, 1548. This is possibly the earliest printed illustration showing cheese-making.

The Bell Inn, Stilton, from a drawing by Herbert Railton, *c.* 1880.

The advent of the railways altered the Stilton cheese industry immediately. Its success as an internationally recognized cheese rested solely on its availability in London. The railway system allowed more of the London aristocracy to visit Melton Mowbray in support of the local hunts, and once they had discovered this cheese, they promoted it to an enormous extent. Railway wagons were filled with Stilton cheese for transporting to London on a weekly basis, with some special deliveries made direct to the Houses of Parliament.

Stilton has been a popular cheese in the British Isles since its standardization at the beginning of the eighteenth century. Until the building of specialized dairies at the end of the nineteenth century, it was always very localized. Hundreds of farmers' wives made Stilton with their surplus milk, often producing only one or two cheeses per day. These would be sold at various markets, especially fairs in Melton Mowbray, and arrangements would be made with cheese factors for the collection and marketing of cheese. Co-operatives were formed and some farming families amassed considerable wealth through marketing Stilton cheese. One such farmer was Henry Morris of Saxelbye, who in 1910 owned seven dairies producing Stilton cheese. A number of specialized dairies were built before the First World War and many of these still produce cheese today.

In this book I have compiled an account of how I consider Stilton cheese to have developed – a word I use advisedly. Like so many types of food and commodities, Stilton developed – it was not invented, it did not appear overnight. Farmers' wives in Little Dalby and Withcote, and the cook at Quenby Hall, have all been credited in various historic accounts as making the first Stilton cheese. That they made a blue-veined cream cheese to their own unique recipe is not in dispute. It was their own recipe that they recorded! Today, each of the seven dairies producing Stilton cheese uses its own recipe – not one dairy produces Stilton cheese in exactly the same way as its competitors. The same basic formula is used, but each dairy produces its own unique cheese.

Early accounts of the manufacture of Stilton cheese are scanty. Fortunately, the commercialization of the product, away from the small dairies run by farmers' wives and daughters, occurred contemporaneously with the advent of photography. In these pages I have put together a collection of photographs which, complemented by accompanying text, engravings and drawings, constitutes a record of how I consider the 'King of Cheeses' was developed.

This is my collection, made possible only through the help of very many people. I take full responsibility for the presentation and trust the reader will enjoy my account of the development of the Stilton cheese industry.

Trevor Hickman
September 1995
New edition October 2005

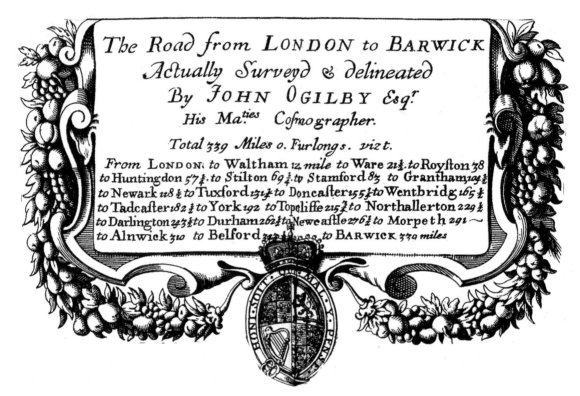

A cartouche from John Ogilby's Atlas of 1675, which shows the small town of Stilton on the Great North Road. On this map, Stilton is sixty-nine and a quarter miles north of London.

1

A Historical Survey

Cheese has probably been made in England for well over four thousand years. The first cheese makers would have been the early farmers of the Neolithic period (between *c.* 4000 and 2400 BC), and the first cheese was probably made by accident. According to the few written observations that have survived, cheese first appeared in the Middle East, possibly in the area now comprising Turkey and Iran. Did some wandering traveller place his daily supply of milk in a bag made of animal skin with some offal still inside it, mount his beast of burden and travel along the highway, with the animal's movement and the hot sun separating the curd from the whey, and the liquid draining out through a hole in the bag? Was this how the first crude cheese was produced?

Cheese is mentioned in Greek mythology while the earliest written reference goes back nearly six thousand years. It is referred to in the book of Samuel in the Bible. Saul is fighting the Philistines and Jesse tells his son David to take food to his brothers: 'and carry these ten cheese unto the captain of their thousand'. Cheese was part of the staple diet of the marching Roman legions, the Mediterranean invaders that conquered and occupied England for almost four hundred years. It is repeatedly referred to in Roman cookery books. Archaeological surveys have indicated that north-east Leicestershire was farmed by numerous Romano-British communities. They would have raised cows, goats and sheep, and made cheese.

Cream cheese would have been made by the very first farmers who planted their crops and reared their cattle and sheep on the fertile fields of the Midlands. Neolithic man farmed in what is now the parish of Wymondham. A Neolithic polished stone axe-head was discovered on the outskirts of the village in 1975 and subsequently dated to *c.* 2500 BC, while a saddle quern of the same period, used for grinding corn, was recovered at Grange Farm in 1976. This indicates a stable farming community, who would have grazed cattle and sheep, sown crops and made cheese. Aerial surveys have indicated that an Iron Age farming community worked the land in the parish of Wymondham, and two Roman villa sites have also been located there. This pattern of farming activity would have been duplicated throughout the rolling heathlands of the north-east Midlands and is not unique to Wymondham. Emphasis has been placed on the parish of Wymondham because most researchers who comment on the origins of Stilton cheese arrive at the conclusion that a blue-veined cream cheese could have been produced in this part of Leicestershire since records began.

Such blue-veined cream cheese is considered to be nearly as old as cheese itself. The story of the introduction of Roquefort could have a parallel in the production of the first Stilton cheese. Legend has it that a group of French peasants were grazing their flocks high up in the Cevennes mountains (where this famous French cheese is still made) when they were surprised by some brigands who drove off their flocks. The shepherds fled, returning days later to look for their abandoned *fromagen*, a soft cheese made from ewes' milk and bread. Their frugal meal was still hidden where they had left it and had developed a firm crust with blue mould running through the mixture. Their hunger pangs were so great that they made a meal out of what had survived, and found it very palatable. Thus Roquefort was born. This was a cheese that the Romans ate, and no doubt a cream cheese was also available in the farms at Wymondham. In fact, the Romans exported cheese from England to Rome.

Cheese is derived from the Latin word *caseus*. In England, before AD 1100, it was called *cyse* and later became *cease*; in the sixteenth and seventeenth centuries, *ches* and *chiese*. The earliest written reference book mentioning cheese in England was compiled by the master of cooks to Richard II in 1390, as a manuscript volume of recipes entitled *The Forme of Cury, a Roll of Ancient English Cookery*. It was first published as a printed book in 1781, and contains a recipe to add grated cheese to soup.

To produce good quality milk, the correct type of soil is essential, and the best cheese has always been made from the milk of cows that graze on good pasture. Without good grass, it is impossible to obtain the quality and above all the quantity that is so necessary to produce fine cream cheese. The first domesticated cattle were of a different breed to those encountered today, being semi-wild with small udders. The Romans bred new strains, but after they left Britain they had no influence on subsequent agricultural change and development. The Saxons and Danes farmed the East Midlands fields for nearly seven hundred years, and certainly considered cheese to be an important part of their diet. The Scandinavian invaders introduced a breed of cattle into England which eventually gave rise to the strain known as Lincoln Reds. These cattle are noted for their size and hardiness, and are dual-purpose cattle raised for beef production and seasonal milk yields. It was this breed that became the cow of the Leicestershire and Lincolnshire wolds.

The next major development came with the Norman Conquest in 1066, following which William the Conqueror divided up England, granting vast areas of his new kingdom to his victorious generals. They in their turn endowed large tracts of farming land to provide support to various religious establishments, abbeys, monasteries, priories and churches, throughout England. Many religious houses were built in the Midlands, including, in the area around Melton Mowbray, at Croxton Kerrial, Laund and Kirby Bellars. Of these three Kirby Bellars has the most significance, with evidence of cheese manufacture in a dairy attached to the priory at an early

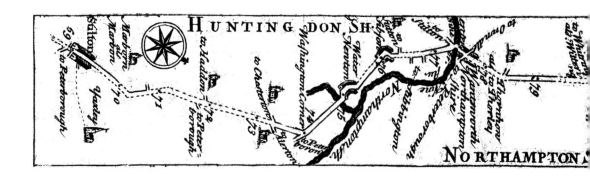

Two strip maps from *Britannia Depicta* engraved by Emanuel Bowen in 1720, taken from Ogilby's maps of 1675. Bowen's maps were reproduced in the first pocket-size road atlas ever published, to be carried in large pockets by post boys who travelled the highways of England, delivering mail.

date. Supporting evidence is provided by the walled enclosures, erected by the monks for rearing cows, which still stand next to the main Leicester–Melton Mowbray road. No doubt all monastic buildings operating in a farming area would have included a dairy, as would houses built for the families of the local nobility.

Cheese was an essential food throughout the medieval period. All the religious houses would be liable to receive tithe and taxes, paid into their system of administration to support their work with the poor and assist in maintaining Christianity in an agricultural district. Cheese made from surplus milk by any villager who could support a cow, and from the cows and large flocks of sheep owned by the lord of the manor, would have been an easy commodity to transport as tithe: it would not deteriorate to the same extent as other edible products and as it aged it often improved in quality. Friars and monks attached to the religious houses more often than not served as farm labourers; they reared cows for milk and would certainly have had a surplus which would be made into cheese. Because hospitality was part of most monastic orders, cheese would be offered as standard fare for all travellers and incumbents residing in religious establishments in this area of the Midlands. It is hardly likely that any form of milk collection existed, and all milk would have been produced on site. Were the monks and friars influenced by the lords of the various manors who were paying dues to them? Possibly so! There is no written survey available to indicate that any farmland capable of rearing milking cows in the Melton Mowbray area took precedence over any other parish in the district, but written evidence suggests that the parish of Wymondham was a district that contained fine pasture, suitable for rearing milking cows and very large flocks of sheep towards the end of the medieval period. It also had a direct link with Kirby Bellars Priory, as had the adjacent villages of Garthorpe and Stapleford.

On 31 August 1319 Sir John Hamelin was one of the witnesses to the charter founding the chantry that was later to become the priory of Kirby Bellars, endowed by Roger Bellars. The Hamelin family had farmed the Wymondham lands, some 480 acres, since the 1150s as tenants of the Ferrars family, headed by the earls of Derby, who were granted the land by William the Conqueror. Eventually the Hamelins were established as overlords in their own right, by right of purchase and decree. The lord of the manor of Wymondham continued to support the religious establishment at Kirby Bellars until the suppression of the monasteries in the sixteenth century.

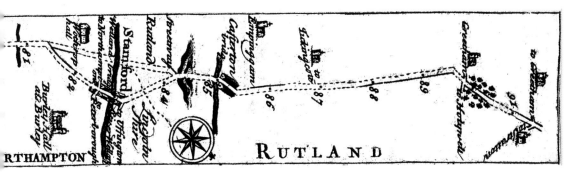

Each map detailed landmarks that could be viewed from the back of a horse being ridden along the highway. Yaxley church tower was such a reference point, on the approach to Stilton from the south.

The animals that produced the milk in sufficient quantity for cheese to be made during the medieval period were most probably ewes. Vast flocks of sheep roamed the rolling plains of the shire counties, some contained in hurdles on common land. Though this cannot be proved conclusively, cheese was certainly a seasonal product, controlled by natural forces such as drought and famine years. The terrible famine that devastated the Midlands in 1316 would have decimated the sheep and cattle populations of the shires, and it would have taken decades to recover from the disaster. Very little cheese of any kind was available as there was no surplus milk. It is fairly certain that the cheese produced was small in size and in weight, not unlike the 'baby Stiltons' that are marketed today, made from ewes' and cows' milk. These early cheeses were unpressed, the curd being wrapped in linen cloths and the whey squeezed out, then the pouches hung up to drain. To speed up the process, weights were placed on the cloth bags that were stacked on shelves, thus ensuring the whey drained away more quickly. This method was eventually superseded by a purpose-built press. Unpressed cheese was made side by side with pressed cheese, and unpressed cheese developed blue mould very quickly between the crumbled curds. The curd eventually was packed into a hoop and stacked on a hastener.

In the village of Wymondham some farmers made pressed cheese, while others made unpressed. A distinctive type of unpressed cheese developed, and was marketed with a variety of names until it was called 'Stilton cheese' in about 1700.

Established religious houses at this time supported only one or two milking cows. Quite possibly it was not until the reign of Henry VII, commencing in 1485, that considerable change took place. This king encouraged trade not war, and country districts became more stable. The monastic orders became involved in village administration to an enormous extent, gaining wealth and power. Their involvement in producing and marketing food so increased that it was one of the contributing factors to their eventual downfall.

Under the feudal system, the Hamelin family, as lords of the manor and the farmers of Wymondham, organized the tilling of the soil, rotation of crops, and the raising of animals for slaughter and milk production. Tithes were paid to the overlord and to the religious houses in turn. Kirby Bellars was one of these, and that the Hamelins had a direct financial link with this priory is a well-recorded fact. However, their involvement with property in Huntingdonshire has more relevance to this account of cheese manufacture.

The last of the line of the Wymondham Hamelins was Isobel, the daughter of Sir John Hamelin. She married Thomas Berkeley in about 1290. In her marriage settlement, not only were the Wymondham properties to become part of the Berkeley estate, but also sizeable holdings of farmland – approximately 300 acres – in Welde (Weald) and Eynesbury in Huntingdonshire. These Huntingdonshire estates had been under the ownership of the Hamelin family since the late twelfth century, and were to be controlled by the Wymondham Berkeleys until 1574. From the Hamelins of the twelfth century to the Berkeleys in the late sixteenth century, we have 400 years of trade and movement of farming produce, animals and administrators between two farming districts in Leicestershire and Huntingdonshire. These two counties are some distance apart, but are linked by the major roadway that ran from London to Scotland: Ermine Street, the Great North Road. This Roman road, an important highway, passed through the length of Huntingdonshire and ran less than two miles from the eastern boundaries of the parish of Wymondham. The town of Stilton was one of the main terminuses on this highway; for centuries, drovers, pedlars, pack-horse trains and marching armies passed through this small town, or obtained rest and shelter, or refreshed themselves and their animals. The movement of goods for 400 years between the three manorial holdings by pack-horse and stage wagons would have required food to be carried for the long journeys. Bread and cheese have always been the main source of sustenance for the working Englishman and would most certainly have been the fare carried by the travellers between the Berkeleys' farm holdings.

Eynesbury and Welde were not enclosed until 1797, so cow pastures were not available until well into the nineteenth century. This area was noted for sheep grazing. In 1086 it is recorded in the Domesday Book that 662 sheep were contained in the sheep-fold. Ewes' milk would have been used to produce a seasonal cheese and was possibly one of the early cheeses on offer at Stilton, along with similar cheeses from Wymondham.

When was the first inn established in England that can be considered a strictly commercial venture and not a religious rest-house? Possibly as early as the twelfth century, when barns and outbuildings were requisitioned for crusaders on their way to the Holy Land. Marching crusaders certainly passed through junction towns such as Stilton. Records exist of a contingent being formed at Stamford for the third crusade and marching down Ermine Street to London. William Hamelin, knight of Wymondham, took part in this adventure, which commenced in 1189 under the leadership of King Richard I. He would surely have left Wymondham, journeyed down Ermine Street and visited his Huntingdonshire estates on the way. Was there a direct link with a hostelry at Stilton at this early date? Such an establishment would provide a resting place and some food for the weary travellers, the simplest form of food being cheese. Where did the

This illustration was published in Richard Dansey's *The English Crusaders*. It shows the twenty-three knights who accompanied Robert, Earl of Leicester, on the third crusade to the Holy Land in 1189. Nine senior knights, including Robert, are on horseback, with fifteen lesser knights marching on foot with their troops. These troops would have been recruited from within the manorial holding of each knight. It is virtually certain that these men would have regarded cheese as a staple part of their diet. William Hamelin (number XXI), who displayed the arms *chequy*, *argent* and *azure*, would have recruited his band of followers from Wymondham and other parishes in which he had an interest.

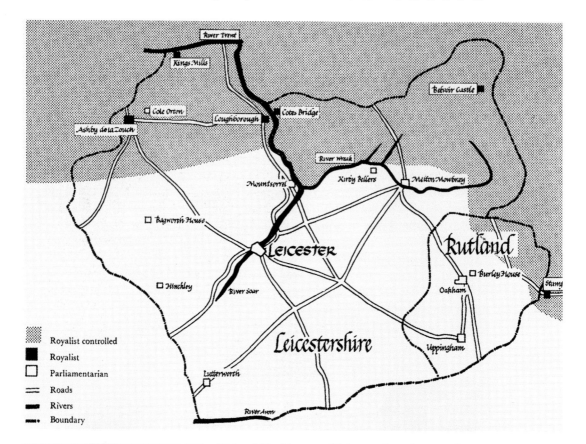

Richard Black's map of Leicestershire showing the areas controlled by the Parliamentarian and Royalist forces during the Civil War. The eastern cheese-producing district of Wymondham came under Royalist control. Kirby Bellars came under Parliamentarian control.

The remains of the manor house built at Colston Bassett by Francis and Margaret Hacker. The inscription on the chimney-stack reads FHMH 1625. Their eldest son, Colonel Francis Hacker, fought for the Parliamentarian cause during the Civil War, and occupied Kirby Bellars Manor House (see p. 82), with its cheese-producing dairy. For a few years he owned land in the village of Stathern in the Vale of Belvoir. Could this be one of the reasons why this district has become one of the recognized areas of the East Midlands where Stilton cheese developed and is still produced in large quantities at four dairies?

The main mode of travel for any distance on the highways of England until the end of the eighteenth century was horseback. Because of the state of the highways, travel by coach was extremely uncomfortable and difficult, and above all it was expensive. This drawing shows the commonest form of travel for a family: a large shire horse fitted with two panniers. The squire, his lady and his daughter travel at a comfortable trot, possibly covering no more than twenty miles per day and resting overnight at hostelries conveniently situated along the highway.

'A Wayside Halt', after Rowlandson. This picturesque scene shows a stage wagon drawn by eight horses leaving a wayside inn. Horses provided the main form of transport along the Great North Road for centuries, through riding on horseback, or having goods transported by stage wagons or pack-horse trains.

cheese come from? It could have been made locally in small quantities. The land to the east of Stilton was fenland, totally unsuitable for rearing sheep and cattle. To the west were hills, unsuitable as grazing land because of the underlying nature of the soil, which produced poor quality grass; it was principally a sheep-grazing area. A ready trade link, however, existed with the cheese-producing district of east Leicestershire. Cheese was most certainly offered in trade, possibly as payment for board and lodgings. There is no way of establishing what type of cheese was available; it would vary to a degree that did not warrant any record being made of its type. A hostelry existed in Stilton in 1437, and along with wine and beer, cheese was on offer. How much of the cream cheese that found its way to Stilton was of the blue-veined variety? A considerable quantity, made from both ewes' and cows' milk.

The milk used to produce Stilton cheese is obtained from cows, and the cows must be reared and live in the correct environment. The countryside around Melton Mowbray is ideal. Which members of the farming community first utilized cows' milk to make cream cheese exclusively? It is not possible to make a positive statement on this. Research has shown, however, that Kirby Bellars Priory could have been the home of a cream cheese from the fourteenth century onwards. Cheese would have been made by the priory's labourers and manufactured in Wymondham simultaneously.

The Berkeleys were also keen farmers and added to their land, establishing farming controls. In the 1560s they set about enclosing the common land in the parish of Wymondham by building walls and ditching and hedging it for their own use. Essentially for the rearing of cattle, it allowed more control of the cows and selective breeding. Better feeding methods from fodder produced in managed meadows led to higher yields of milk, and thus cheese production increased. Maurice Berkeley controlled more cattle than any of his forebears. A number of villagers petitioned the king against these restrictive measures, to no avail. The open-field system was still in operation in the parishes close to Melton Mowbray and to the south, but this method of farming was not conducive to producing surplus milk. The situation did not change until the Enclosure Acts of the 1760s. J. Houghton, in his book *A Collection for the Importance of Husbandry and Trade*, published in 1727, states: 'Among them [cows] a great many small ones, which are hardly worth the keeping, but the encouragement is, and many pernicious commons we have which, for the flush of milk in a few summer months, makes the poor buy cows, to starve them in winter, and to spend so much time running after them, as would earn twice the worth of their milk by an ordinary manufacture; when as, if the commons were enclosed, some would feed them well all summer . . . whereby there would always be a tolerable plenty of milk, from which would spring many more considerable dairies.'

When the royal commissioner visited the priory in 1536, the records showed that there were in the employment of the prior, sixteen yeomen, seventeen field labourers and a dairy woman. King Henry VIII closed down Kirby Bellars Priory a few months later. Following this more villagers were undoubtedly involved in cheese production. The following list is included in the probate inventory of John Andrews of Kirby Bellars, dated 25 January 1640:

In the Dairy
One cheese presse one churne two tubbes, three pales, panchions three and other small things there. In the chamber over the dairy, cheses, chesebords, bacon and other small things.

Most of the priory building was demolished after dissolution and the remaining portion was altered to form the manor house. In 1573 Thomas Markham purchased the land including the dissolved priory and enclosed a further eighty acres of arable land in 1593, converting it to

An engraving of 'The High Flyer' in 1812, after a painting by J. Emery. This famous coach travelled non-stop from London to Edinburgh, in two days and three nights, only stopping to change horses, drivers and guards. It offered refreshment to the passengers at such hostelries as The Bell at Stilton.

A familiar sight in High Leicestershire during the interwar years and the 1950s: milk churns, containing on average 17 gallons of milk, waiting to be collected by their respective dairies. One churn represented one Stilton cheese, with 17 gallons of milk making a 16 lb cheese – the recommended standard weight.

pastures. Eventually all the land passed to the de la Fontaine family. By 1603 Sir Erasmus de la Fontaine held the manor and lived in the mansion house built on the site of the priory in the middle of the seventeenth century. He supported Charles I during the Civil War and in 1643 Kirby Bellars manor house was occupied by Parliamentarian troops under the command of Colonel Francis Hacker of Colston Bassett in Nottinghamshire. On 25 February 1646 a skirmish took place there. Most of the house was burnt to the ground. Hacker fled, owing to the superiority of the cavalry commanded by Marmaduke Langdale, and the manor was soon recaptured by Parliament forces. Wymondham, however, came under the control of the Royalists (see map on p. 16).

A supply problem existed between east Leicestershire and the town of Stilton, and movement of troops between Cromwell's headquarters in Huntingdonshire and Kirby Bellars would have taken place. Scavengers for food were some of the main participants, as camp-followers and auxiliary troops in the make-up of both armies during the Civil War. It could have been at this time that the traditional shaped strong-tasting cream cheese made from cows' milk arrived at Stilton. Trade had increased to such an extent that it warranted a major restoration of The Bell, completed in 1642, as recorded on a date stone set high up on the building. The Civil War would have increased trade even more.

The Berkeley estates in Wymondham had been sold in 1635 to the Sedleys, whose main home was in Kent. The Sedleys 'sat on the fence' during the Civil War. From their estate map of Wymondham, drawn in 1652, it is clear that they attached considerable importance to farming the land, and they must have produced quantities of cheese, using surplus milk from cows reared in the fields enclosed by the Berkeleys during the previous century. Again we have a continuous trading link down the Great North Road. Even though the country was ravaged by war, trade continued. Cheese represented a source of easily transported food that became important at Stilton during the Civil War but distribution did not peak until the 1840s. Cheese was supplied from the parts of Leicestershire that were under Parliamentary control during the conflict. Quantity was the main criterion. Dairies producing cheese, such as those at Kirby Bellars and Wymondham, were requisitioned to supply the hungry troops. Bulk movement was important and cheese could be produced in larger units for ease of transportation. It is likely that, as a result of demand, the drum-shaped cream cheese arrived for sale at Stilton. It was possibly first made at Kirby Bellars, but then also in the farm dairies at Wymondham. From the 1560s onwards, there is evidence in probate inventories covering the estates of deceased farmers in the parish of Wymondham that indicates a thriving cheese-producing community, manufacturing pressed and unpressed cream cheese.

The Sedley farms could easily have supplied both sides during the Civil War. Their cheeses were sold alongside all other cheeses of different consistencies and make, and of all shapes and sizes. Hungry troops would not differentiate between the cheeses. After the end of the war, when the country became more stable, supplies could have been maintained through the Sedley estate at Wymondham. Colonel Francis Hacker, who had occupied Kirby Bellars Manor House, was a close confidant of Oliver Cromwell. Was he instrumental in introducing a specific type of cheese to Stilton as opposed to the random selection that was available? Did he introduce direct supply lines from an area to the south and east of Melton Mowbray during the Civil War, which were maintained and expanded during Cromwell's Interregnum of 1649–60? It must always be remembered that the eventual victors write the history. It would not be politically expedient to hand any credit to Colonel Hacker after the Restoration; in fact most references to the man would have been destroyed. He escorted Charles I to his execution in 1649, was declared a traitor on Charles II's victorious return to England, and was hanged at Tyburn in 1660. He lived

Left: container for producing starter milk, with thermometer. Right: curd ladle used to transfer curd into a linen strainer.

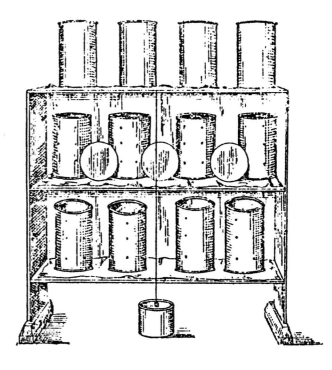

Wooden hastener with hoops, 1889. Metal hoops were hand packed with crumbled curd. They were then stacked in a hastener, the weight of the curd pressing out the whey. This drained through a series of channels cut into the shelves on the hastener, to be collected in a container that was placed under the centre of the bottom shelf. The hoops containing the curd were continuously turned until all the whey had drained out.

at the manor house at Colston Bassett, which, along with the estate, was forfeited on his execution, although it was purchased by his younger brother Rowland, a captain in the army of Charles I. Colston Bassett is a village with a long record of cheese manufacture. Did Francis Hacker employ people to make a blue-veined cream cheese in a dairy on his estate?

With the Restoration of the monarchy in 1660, the country entered a new age. Sir Charles Sedley, a favourite of Charles II, owned the Wymondham farmlands and in 1665 it is on record that he maintained a fine house, his cellar holding the best French wines. No doubt he also served his own superb cheese at his own table. As the country again became stable, discrimination entered into the type of cheese required at The Blue Bell at Stilton. Also after the Restoration, long-distance trade began to increase on the roads that began to be improved under Cromwell's rule, and gathered pace under the various acts of Parliament introduced during Charles II's reign.

Cheese production was developing around Melton Mowbray. Sir Erasmus de la Fontaine had reoccupied Kirby Bellars manor house and no doubt encouraged the production of his speciality cheese. His daughter Mary married Thomas Beaumont, and was a constant visitor to Quenby Hall, some seven miles from her parental home. Here, in a friendly gesture, she passed on the recipe for making a strong-tasting cream cheese to the Ashby family, who, as farmers, were developing the production of cheese in their large dairy, which still stands at Quenby Hall. This cheese was called Lady Beaumont's cheese and was made by Miss Elizabeth Scarborough, who worked in the dairy at the hall. She later married a Mr Orton of Little Dalby. An eighteenth-century record states that there was at Quenby 'species of cheese made for family use, under the name of Lady Beaumont's cheese, and that in size and shape it was much like a "child's Bartholomew-fair drum".' It was a pressed cheese and by today's standards could not be classed as a Stilton cheese. But like so many cheeses made at this time, as it matured blue mould formed inside the crust. This type of cheese was probably already on offer for sale in the town of Stilton, along with unpressed cream cheeses; because of demand, every farmhouse with dairy facilities would produce quantities of cream cheese under a variety of names.

Sir Charles Sedley (the last of the Wymondham Sedleys) had parted with his Wymondham estate by 1700. However, as a confidant of Charles II, a Member of Parliament and a man of some business acumen, he must have ensured that produce from his farm holdings in Leicestershire was sold in the town of Stilton, which he passed through on many occasions on his way to London and Kent. He probably stayed overnight at The Blue Bell Inn. He certainly could not have travelled more than a hundred miles from London to Wymondham without resting on the way.

With the turn of the eighteenth century, the cheese trade at Stilton gathered momentum. Cheese would have been obtained from a variety of sources, possibly haphazardly and, with demand increasing, from all possible suppliers. The first published reference to a cheese called 'Stilton' is made in William Stukeley's *Itinerarium Curiosum*, letter V, October 1722. That it was a seasonal product was confirmed by Professor Richard Bradley in his survey of 1727, when he refers to the famous Stilton cheese being offered at The Blue Bell Inn in the town. In addition, two lines of verse from Pope's Satire VI, *Imitation of Horace*, published in 1738, clearly date a cheese called Stilton:

Cheese such as men in Suffolk make,
But wished it Stilton for his sake.

It was clearly the premier cheese then!

William Pawlett, a native of the village of Market Overton in Rutland, lived and farmed near the Great North Road. As an enterprising businessman, he must have been aware of the enormous potential for marketing Stilton cheese. In 1742 he married Frances, a widow who by

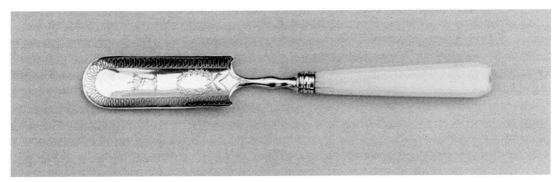

An early example of a Stilton scoop, special spoons introduced in the late eighteenth century. This solid silver scoop with an ivory handle was made in 1802 at Birmingham, during the reign of George III, 'Farmer George', who took a keen interest in English agriculture.

A 1930s Stilton cheese server, in the shape of a trowel. As Stilton cheese became universally more popular and was no longer served just to a select few, so the method of serving changed. For the majority of people, presenting half a Stilton after a meal was not acceptable. Stilton was sold in wedges, and therefore a cheese knife was all that was needed. If a half Stilton is presented on a dining table, the cheese should be cut like cake in neat wedges, not scooped out. This allows the cheese to be stored properly and prevents excessive drying out. Like good red wine, Stilton should be served at normal room temperature, so highlighting its blue veining, creamy texture and unique taste.

Overleaf:
Cary's 'New and Correct Map of Huntingdonshire', published in its final state in 1875, and showing Ermine Street, Stilton Fen, the recently built railway system and the villages of Eynesbury and Welde near St Neots. These are all very important features in the early development of the Stilton cheese trade.

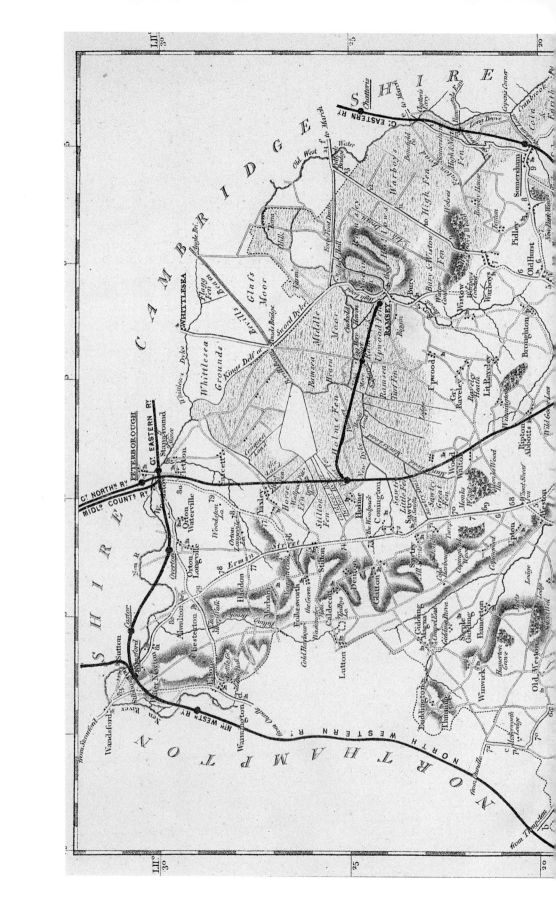

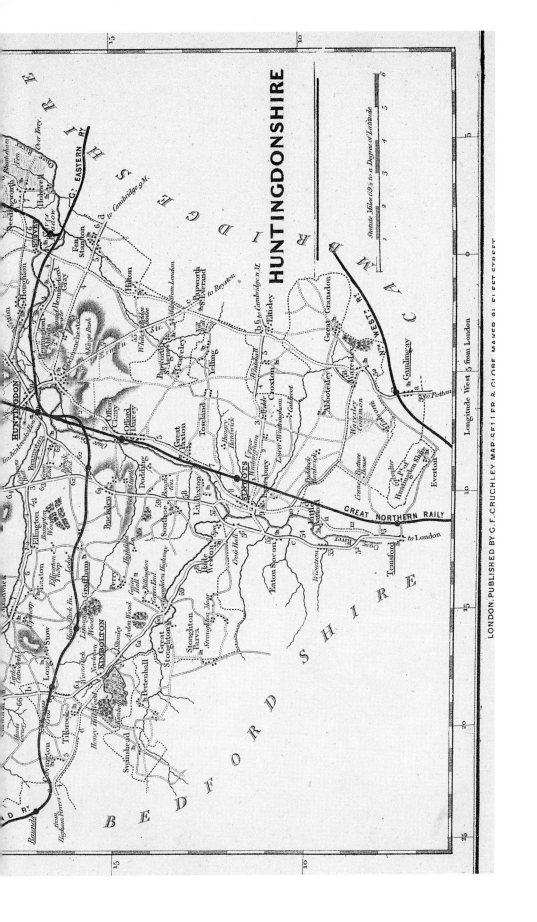

HUNTINGDONSHIRE

LONDON, PUBLISHED BY G. F. CRUCHLEY, MAP-SELLER & GLOBE MAKER 81, FLEET STREET

Statute Miles 69½ to a Degree of Latitude

Longitude West 5 from London

this time had established herself as a supreme cheese-maker, producing fine quality blue-veined cream cheese. Frances's skill, combined with William's business acumen, led to the Pawletts setting up the first cheese marketing co-operative supplying the town of Stilton. For more than forty years the Pawletts' cheese was on sale there. Cooper Thornhill at The Bell entered into a business arrangement with them and wagon-loads of cheese were delivered to Stilton. Possibly the staging area was in Market Overton, a parish very close to the Great North Road.

Legend has it that a certain amount of secrecy was involved with regard to the location of the source of supply of the unique blue-veined cream cheese, marketed exclusively from the town of Stilton. The leading retailers implied that it was made in the town and surrounding district. The travellers who visited the town and considered that the cheese was made locally must have been highly gullible town and city dwellers! Where were the dairies capable of producing the quantities that were being offered for sale?

Not until Charles Colling and Robert Bakewell began breeding experiments in the eighteenth century, assisted by alterations to the methods of feeding cattle introduced by Lord ('Turnip') Townsend (1674–1738), did improved milk yields from cows allow the mass production of cheese. Until the early eighteenth century it was very much a seasonal commodity made from spare milk. Cheese production was expanded throughout the country in the early eighteenth century. It was at this time that the Pawletts saw their opportunity and 'latched on' to the 'Stilton' market, using their own recipe to produce a distinctive cheese in close co-operation with Cooper Thornhill.

The four main hostelries in the town retailed Stilton cheese, and it was also sold by many inns in the locality, especially along the Great North Road. These retailers obtained their supplies from a variety of sources. With stage and posting coaches passing through the town continuously, day and night, changing horses, collecting mail, goods and passengers, trade was enormous. At the peak of its business, the Angel Inn (also owned by Cooper Thornhill from 1743) stabled more than two hundred horses, and was considered to be the leading hostelry in the district. All this came to an abrupt end in the 1840s. The town of Stilton enjoyed a prominent position on the main arterial road of England, particularly following the impact of the industrial revolution that changed the British Isles from the early eighteenth century onwards. Part of the progress was the introduction of the railway throughout the country. The Midland Railway Company connected Peterborough with London and the Midland market towns. The success of Stilton cheese lay in marketing the product in London. Why transport cheese to a small town on the Great North Road, when a direct link now existed? Almost overnight the retail and wholesale business of marketing Stilton cheese collapsed. The stage-coach business disappeared as a direct result of the railways, which provided a much quicker and more reliable service.

Production of Stilton cheese in the nineteenth century continued to gather momentum. There was hardly a village in Leicestershire, Rutland and parts of Lincolnshire and Nottinghamshire that did not have a farm where the cheese was made. These cheeses were sold at the local market on a weekly basis, to be purchased by dealers for selling on. The first factory built solely for the manufacture of Stilton cheese opened in 1875 in the village of Beeby near Leicester. It was soon followed by other organizations that not only made cheese but also acted as factors. Many villages and towns in the four counties had small dairies operating solely as Stilton cheese factories.

At the end of the nineteenth century the production of Stilton cheese was an essential part of the rural economy of the East Midlands. Many people wrote on the subject and advice was given on standardization. One of the finest accounts on production was compiled in 1889: *The Practice*

Engraving from a letterhead, in use *c.* 1830. During the golden age for the marketing of Stilton cheese from the town of Stilton (from the 1790s to the 1840s), many contractors supplied this small town on the Great North Road with Stilton cheese.

Elizabeth Spooner was such an entrepreneur, purchasing Stilton cheese in and around Leicester then conveying it to the Bell Inn at Stilton on a regular basis, using a lightly constructed four-wheeled postillion-driven chaise. This was a very fast carriage, with movable hood. The horses were controlled by the driver riding on the back of the nearside horse.

Thomas Nuttall and Charlotte Fairbrother, cheesemakers from Beeby, at the cheese market in Leicester, 1903. Although the sale of Stilton was dominated by the famous cheese market at Melton Mowbray from 1883 to 1914, Leicester, as well as Nottingham, Derby, Loughborough, Grantham, Oakham and Stamford markets all sold Stilton when surpluses occurred. (Reproduced by kind permission of Leicestershire Museums, Arts and Records Service.)

of Stilton Cheese Making by Mr G. Kemp, a cheese-maker of some renown, who ran his dairy at Manor House Farm, Sedgebrook, near Grantham in Lincolnshire. It was published as a pamphlet by the Royal Agricultural Society of England.

Buildings. – There should be four separate apartments: – the dairy, for setting the milk and draining the curd, which should have temperature of never less than 55° nor more than 60°. It must be fitted with a stove, or hot water heating apparatus, to keep the temperature up in cool weather – 12 feet by 14 feet is a nice size.

The next apartment is the draining-room, where the curd is taken immediately. It is put in the mould (called by cheese-makers the hoop), until such time as it is ready to put in the binder. This room must have a temperature of never less than 63° or more than 67°; 65° is the proper heat. During April and, say, the first two weeks in May, if the heating apparatus is not very perfect, it will be advisable to increase the temperature in these two rooms from 3° to 5°, as the outside temperature varies. *It must be borne in mind that a cheese in the hoop if once starved is spoilt.* The dairy and draining-room must have cement floors and trapped drains; there must be no crevice for the whey to get in, as the odour from stagnant whey is

The Angel Inn, Stilton. This inn figures largely in the early marketing of Stilton cheese. Purchased by Cooper Thornhill in 1743, it became one of the most important hostelries on the Great North Road, dominating the Stilton cheese trade at the turn of the nineteenth century. It had facilities for stabling 300 horses, resident farriers and blacksmiths. In addition, droves of cattle were shod on their way to Smithfield market, and geese had their feet coated in tar. This was achieved by walking the geese through tar, then through sawdust, then through tar again, providing the unfortunate birds with 'shoes' so that their webbed feet did not wear out as they walked to their destiny in the London markets. Some geese did survive their long trip and being sold at the 'Goose Fairs', and the shoe of tar compound eventually fell off.

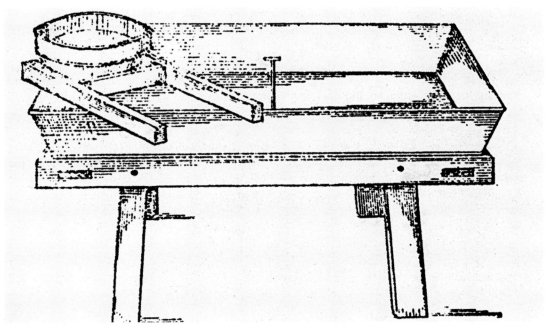

Drawing of a draining trough (lead) used in 1889. The coagulated milk was ladled into this trough very carefully with a shallow bowl, on to a straining cloth. This cloth was then tied as a parcel using all four corners (see photograph on p. 119). The whey then gradually drained away through a controlled outlet in the centre of the trough.

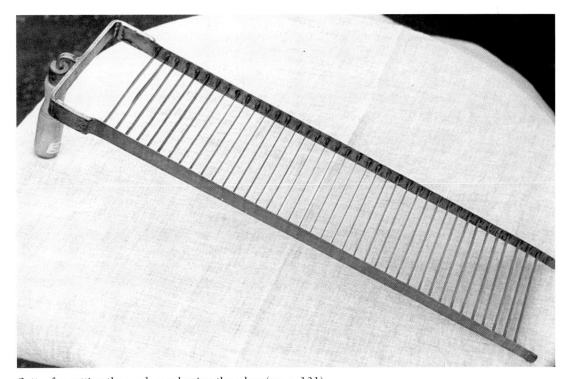

Cutter for cutting the curd, so releasing the whey (see p. 131).

very objectionable, and all offensive smells must be carefully avoided. The size should be 8 feet by 12 feet, and it should have one entrance only, as it is important to keep the temperature of this room very even.

No. 3 is the drying-room, where the cheese is taken after the binder is taken off and the coat is formed. This room (size 14 feet by 10 feet) must have a temperature of from 50° to 55°, and be fitted with windows to open or shut as the draught is required. All windows must have small perforated zinc as well as glass, also inside shutters to exclude the mid-day light. This direction applies to all windows throughout the buildings.

No. 4 is the storing-room (size 14 feet by 24 feet), which should be so contrived as to have regulated draughts. It is a great advantage if the floor is about two feet below the surface of the ground, as the air of this room requires to be somewhat moist. The temperature should range from 50°– 60°; if the cheeses are wanted to ripen quicker it may be raised to 65°, or even a little higher; but it will be well to bear in mind that a quickly ripened cheese will not keep so well when cut as one that has ripened more naturally.

All the buildings should have a northern aspect, and must be protected from the full force of the summer sun; no shade is so good as that of trees.

In the foregoing directions as to buildings it has not been the intention to give a design for a Stilton cheese-making factory, but for such structures as are required for a dairy of about twenty cows, and as a rule attached to the house of an ordinary farmer or grazier.

Utensils. – The utensils required are, in the dairy or setting-room, milk coolers, a setting-pan, strainering, draining-trough, and moulds or hoops, and, if the quantity of curd is large, say, 30 cows – a curd-breaker. The setting-pan is either single or double skinned: if double, the space between the skins can be filled with hot or cold water as needed; if single, it is best made of tinned steel. The single is preferable; it is much handier to clean and to move about. Strainering is the ordinary butter-strainering cut into squares of about 48 inches, and can be obtained of almost any linen draper. The draining-trough is best made of wood lined with sheet-lead, sides rather sloping. It must be fitted with tap to let off the whey, and also a movable perforated tin bottom, raised half an inch to allow the whey to run away freely – size 6 inches deep, 22 inches wide at bottom, and 28 inches wide at top, with a length according to number of cows. The hoops are circular, made of tin, 13 inches high, 8 inches diameter, sides perforated to admit of skewering; if well filled they will make a cheese when ripe of 15 lbs. weight.

Draining-room. – The drainer is of wood, 1 inch thick, 4 feet 3 inches high, 5 feet long, 11 inches from front to back; the front open, the back closed, with top, middle, and bottom shelves – the bottom shelf 1 foot from the floor, the remaining space equally divided. Each shelf must have a groove cut all round, half an inch from the edge to drain off the whey, and a hole through the centre of the front groove through which to pass a string to conduct the whey into a vessel placed under the bottom shelf. A deal table is required to place the cheeses on during the time the drainer is being brushed, washed, and clean cloths put on the shelves.

Manufacture. – In the first place, the milk must be produced by cows fed on good old grass pastures – which ought to have a clay subsoil – supplemented, it may be, by a little cake. Too much cake is not good: about 2 lbs. per cow per day is quite sufficient, unless the pasture is very poor, and then a little more may be given. It is not, however, advisable to attempt Stiltons at all on a very poor pasture, as they are almost sure to be of poor quality. On the other hand, a very rich pasture is to be avoided by all but the most expert cheese-makers, and even by them it is a risky undertaking. But we wish to say that a true Stilton is not made from unskimmed milk only, but has a certain amount of cream added to it.

The
KINGSTON
Cheese
Apparatus

For making
Kingston and
other small
Cheeses.

For Prices and particulars apply

VIPAN & HEADLY,
Dairy Engineers, LEICESTER.

An advertisement published in 1920, showing a 10 lb Stilton hoop and a curd cutter.

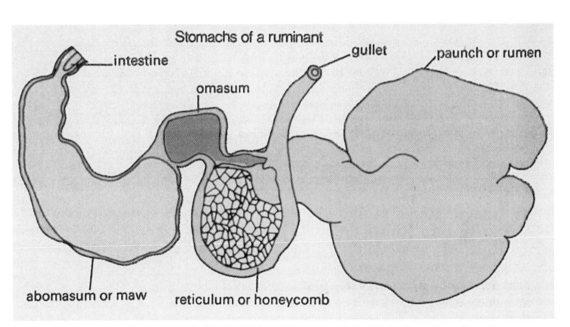

Rennet is the essential agent needed to coagulate milk to produce curd. Rennin is the active enzyme involved, and is found in the stomach walls of mammals, with the greatest concentration being in the rumen of an unweaned calf.

In the 1920s and '30s salted calves' stomachs were imported into England from Poland, packed in small barrels. These 'vels' were then washed to remove excess salt, turned inside out and soaked for a few days. The resulting liquid, the rennet, was then stored in earthenware jars. This form of supply was acceptable to the large manufacturers of cheese, while many small farm dairies still purchased calves' paunches direct from the local slaughterhouse, for immediate use.

The evening's milk is cooled to 65° at the time of milking by means of Lawrence's refrigerator, and set until morning in a tin vessel 8 inches deep, 28 inches wide, and 40 inches long, having a hole in the bottom closed with a plug, the stem of which is long enough to stand above the milk when the vessel is full. It must rest on a wood frame 18 inches high, to admit of a bucket being placed underneath in which to draw off the milk.

In the morning draw off one-sixth of the milk through the plug hole and put it out of the way (this should not be put in the setting-pan); then draw off a tin bucketful and immerse it in hot water till it is raised to 110°, stirring occasionally to prevent skimming on the top. Pour it in the setting-pan, draw off another bucketful, and treat in the same way until the vessel is empty. The cream which is left to last must not be raised more than 98°. Add the whole of the morning's milk after it has been drawn from the cows half an hour, care being taken that the cream does not rise on the new milk – this can be prevented by an occasional slight stirring.

The milk in the setting-pan should be 84° or 86°, according as the outside temperature is high or low at the time the rennet is added. Be careful to mix thoroughly; cover the pan with a light cloth to prevent the heat escaping. Home-made rennet is usually employed, but Hansen's rennet tablets answer equally well, though they are more costly. Any one who is not able to make his own rennet is strongly advised to use the tablets, as they are very clean and simple, full directions for use being given with each package.

The manufacture of rennet was one of the well-kept secrets involved in Stilton cheese production. Traditionally the stomach lining from the rumen of an unweaned calf that is still suckling is steeped in brine, and the enzymes that are present in the tissue are retained in the solution. This liquid is then stored in a brown glass or earthenware jar for use as required. At no time must rennet be exposed to the sun or the enzymes will be killed, making the agent useless. Today rennet is made from vegetable products, producing cheese acceptable to vegetarians. In 1727 a rennet was produced by boiling goose grass, *Galium aparine*, in water.

The milk will be coagulated in from ten to fifteen minutes. In two and a half hours from setting, the curd will be ready to put in the draining-trough; this is done by gently ladling, with a shallow tin bowl holding about half a gallon, the whole contents of the setting-pan into the draining-trough (rods of iron or wood must be placed across the top of the draining-trough to carry the edges of the strainering), in which a piece of wet strainering about 48 inches square has been previously placed to receive it. One piece of strainering will hold the curd of about seven gallons of milk.

When the curd is all in the draining-trough, tie the four corners of the strainering loosely together: let the whey stop in the trough half or three-quarters of an hour before drawing off. The curd must then be tied closer together; this is done by placing the four corners of the strainering together.

In tying up the curd grasp the strainer with the left hand close to the curd, and with the right hand take one of the loose corners and bind the whole tightly together under the left hand. This apparently simple operation will require some practice before it can be neatly and deftly done. Very great care must be taken not to crush the curd at any time, or the whey will run white, which must not be allowed. The main object is to keep the whey as green as possible.

The tying will want repeating three or four times during the day, until the curd is sufficiently firm to cut into blocks the size of half a brick, which will be from six to seven

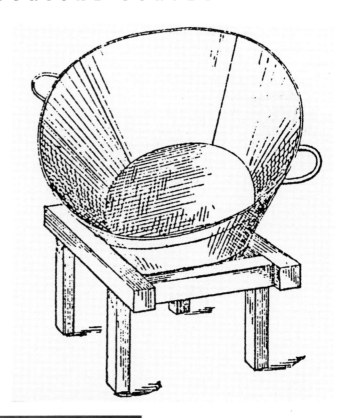

Making up pan, 1889.

A steel-rimmed hoop standing on a 'bit and board' in a draining tray, used by United Dairies in the village of Harby. Tom Dickman of Harby was a fine tinsmith and made all the 'Harby hoops' during the 1920s and '30s.

hours from ladling. The pieces must be carefully turned over, and the whole covered with a light cotton cloth the following morning. It is now ready to put in the mould (or hoop), but before doing so, the pieces must be broken to the size of a walnut, mixing salt in the proportion of 8 ozs. of salt to 30 lbs. of curd. When the hoop is being filled, the curd in the hoop should be occasionally lightly pressed with the hand, and when full it must at once be taken to the draining-room and put in the drainer. Before commencing to fill the hoop it will be necessary to place it (the hoop) upon a piece of board, on which to carry it to the drainer; a sinker made of wood, and just sufficiently large to pass easily inside the mould, being placed on the top of curd. As a rule, no other weight should be used, though sometimes it is necessary to do so. No directions as to weights can safely be given: the knowledge must be gained by experience and observation.

After standing three hours, the mould containing the cheese must be turned over on its opposite end, the sinker again being placed on the top. This must be repeated at regular intervals three times a day. At each time of turning on the second and two or three succeeding days the cheese must be skewered through the perforations in the sides of the hoop with a steel skewer about twice the thickness of an ordinary knitting-pin: the outside of the mould containing the cheese must be washed with tepid water, and the drainer thoroughly brushed and washed with hot water every morning.

If the temperature (65°) has been kept even, and the turning and skewering properly attended to, the cheese will be ready for the binder about six days from making. Here again no precise instructions can be given. The cheese should feel rather elastic under pressure of the fingers; it will also have left the sides of the mould slightly, so that the latter easily slips off. When you are satisfied the cheese is ready for the binder – which is a piece of calico as broad as the cheese is high, and an inch or two longer than will encircle it – place the mould containing the cheese on a table, take off the mould, and with an ordinary table-knife commence to fill up the little holes in the sides of the cheese by slowly drawing the flat side of the knife up and down, applying a slight pressure in doing so, till all the holes are filled up and the side of the cheese is smooth and even.

The binder is now tightly pinned around, and the mould, after being thoroughly cleansed, is again placed over the cheese. The next day this binder must be replaced by a clean one, the side of the cheese being again rubbed over with the knife, and the mould replaced. A clean binder must be put on every day, the mould being discarded after the second day. In very drying weather a light covering must be used for all cheeses in binders.

On the first appearance of coat the knife must no longer be used. In about six to eight days the binder will begin to have dry places upon it, which is a sign the coat is beginning to form. To the eye it will look like little white crinkled patches, but in a few days it will spread all over the cheese, and the coat will then be fully formed. The binder must be used until the coat is perfect.

In very damp thundery weather 'slip-cote' – a soft greasy state of the cheese, which will very soon be known by experience – will form instead of the true coat; this must be scraped off with the knife as soon as perceived, and the cheese removed to a cooler place. The best place for the coating process is the setting-dairy, on shelves placed along the wall, except in very hot weather, when a cool moist room is best, with a temperature of about 55°. The storing-room, which at this time is not fully occupied, is a good place, if care is taken to exclude the midday air.

When the coat is fully formed the cheese must be taken to the drying-room, and placed on deal shelves. It now only requires turning every day, and careful attention paid to cleanliness

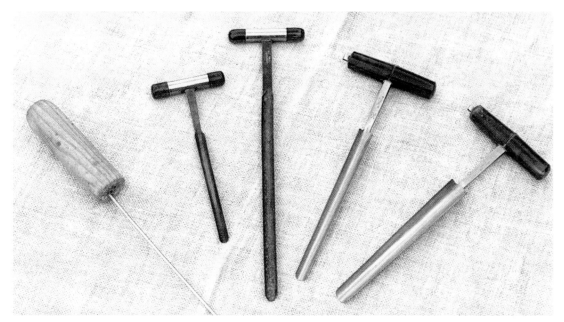

A selection of sampling irons, used for boring holes in the side of maturing cheeses to determine the quality of the product. On the left of this photograph is a home-made piercer used for making small holes in the cheese to speed up the growth of the famous blue mould. These piercers were often made from steel knitting needles.

A Stilton cheese cover commissioned from The London Pottery Co. Ltd by Liam McGivern, landlord of The Bell Inn, Stilton, to commemorate the completion of a major restoration programe of this historic building in 1990. The date on the handle of the cover records another major restoration in 1642. This cover was designed to hold a complete 'baby' Stilton cheese of approximately 8 lb in weight. A mature baby Stilton sits on the plate with the cover removed. The original sixteenth- and seventeenth-century Stiltons would have weighed in at approximately 8–10 lb.

and draughts. The draught should be rather dry and free, but care must be taken that it is not too free, or cracking of the coat will take place, which must be studiously avoided, or the small cheese-fly will deposit its larva in the tiny cracks, and the cheese will be spoilt. The coat should be kept in the same white state as when it came out of the binder. If there is too much moisture in the atmosphere a black mould will form on the coat. This should not be allowed; more dry air must be admitted, and the cheeses placed further apart on the shelves. After it has been in the drying-room about twenty days the coat will be firmly fixed, and the cheese must go to the storing-room, and be ranged in rows on deal shelves. Here it will only require daily turning, the shelves kept quite clean and free from mites, and a careful attention paid to draughts and temperature. In summer the light will have to be excluded at midday.

A Stilton is generally ready for the table in about six months from making. When ready for the table it should have a crinkled light drab coat, it should cut easily with a knife, and if bored it should leave some of the rich soft cheese upon the surface of the borer. It should be well veined with blue, and have a flavour and aroma not to be found in any other cheese of the British or foreign make.

During the First World War consumers witnessed a decline in production. From the 1920s consolidation of manufacture took place, again to be interrupted by the Second World War, when Stilton cheese was considered a non-essential commodity. Wartime restrictions continued until the 1950s. It was in this decade that the cheese industry began to break out of recession and it has continued to grow ever since. The 'King of Cheeses' is now recognized as one of the world's premier blue-veined cream cheeses and is exported from England to most countries in the western world.

It takes on average sixteen gallons of milk to produce one standard Stilton cheese. In converting the milk to curd, half the volume is converted into whey: this is a superb pig food. Many of the Stilton cheese manufacturers raised large herds of pigs and some, like Henry Morris of Saxelbye and Tuxford and Tebbutts invested heavily in the production of the Melton Mowbray pork pie. For further information concerning this famous food consult the author's book *The History of the Melton Mowbray Pork Pie* (Sutton Publishing, 1997).

A wood engraving of a Victorian milk-carriage, patented in 1896, from a drawing by Henry Austin. These carriages were extensively used in the early factory dairies. See the lower photograph on p. 141 of the employees at Hartington, in which a milk-carriage stands to the left.

2

The Town of Stilton

This is not a general history of this small Huntingdonshire (now Cambridgeshire) town. It is an attempt to place on record the reason for one of the most famous cheeses that ever developed – enjoyed by millions of people world-wide – being marketed in this locality. The town of Stilton sits on Ermine Street, the Great North Road, a highway constructed by the Romans, possibly along the line of a prehistoric trackway that skirted the marshes of eastern England. Such long-distance routes as the Great North Road necessitate centres for supplying the needs of the weary traveller. Stilton is such a place, sited about seventy miles from London, a day's journey on horseback or by hard-driven coach. No doubt the fast chariots of Imperial Rome carrying messages to the troop commander on Hadrian's Wall passed this way in the first and second centuries AD. After the fall of the Roman Empire and during the colonization of England by the Saxons, and Scandinavian and Norman invaders, this roadway continued to be the most important highway in England.

In the first detailed map showing the main highways of England, published in 1675 by John Ogilby, Stilton is depicted as a substantial centre on the Great North Road, consisting of two long, stoutly constructed rows of buildings, one on each side of the highway. A hostelry had been operating there in 1437 when Walter Wyghtfeld was sued for not paying his wine bill to an importer operating out of King's Lynn, and records indicate that many inns existed in Stilton, controlled by various religious houses, before the dissolution of the monasteries. In 1501 The Blue Bell Inn was being run by Edward Tebald and in 1503 Margaret Tudor, daughter of Henry VII, stopped in the town, almost certainly at The Blue Bell Inn, on her way north to be married in Edinburgh. The journey was continually interrupted by the poor state of the highway.

During the early sixteenth century, stage wagons came into use, transporting goods alongside pack-horse trains of up to forty animals. These large wagons, drawn by teams of eight horses and travelling at two miles per hour, churned up the highways on long-distance journeys, and smaller versions continued in use as carriers' carts until the early part of the twentieth century. Drovers from the north, destined for Smithfield, also passed through Stilton, achieving twenty miles a day with their sheep, cattle, pigs and geese. One of the major sources of income for blacksmiths in the town was shoeing cattle like horses, and dipping the feet of geese in tar, for the long trek to market. One visit to the town is recorded in *Barnabees Journal*, written in 1618 and published in 1638, which contains a poem, part of which, when translated from the Latin into English verse, reads:

Thence to Stilton, slowly paced
With no bloome nor blossome graced
With no plums nor apples stored
But bald like an Old man's forehead
Yet with Innes so well provided
Guests are pleased when they have tried it.

It is presumed that Barnabee visited Stilton in winter and did not like what seemed to be a bleak fenland town – although the inns were well stocked with ale and cheese.

On 31 July 1635, a proclamation of Charles I commanded that a 'running post' be set up to operate night and day between Edinburgh and London. This required stables to be established to supply fresh horses, and it seems likely that one was set up at Stilton. The Civil War brought considerable disruption to all trade, and many accounts of battles are interspersed with comments on the state of the roads and the difficulty of transporting ordinance to the scene of conflict. However, the close proximity of Cromwell's home and headquarters no doubt boosted the hostelry business in Stilton, and in this way contributed to the development of the type of cheese on offer in the town.

Following the Restoration, Charles II set about improving the road system, an effort that continued under subsequent rulers. A good road system was seen as essential, connecting the industrial north with the city of London. The first turnpike act of 1663 authorized a toll gate to be set up at Stilton, enabling a form of taxation to be levied locally. The responsibility to make up the roads was then the duty of the civic controllers of the town, who were normally trustees to the relevant act and raised the necessary cash by use of such tolls. Road maintenance before this had been very piecemeal. The coaching trade now began to materialize, but most travellers still journeyed on horseback, stopping overnight at The Bell in Stilton and other hostelries in the locality.

Author Daniel Defoe visited Stilton many times and, as a secret agent working in Scotland for King William III between 1697 and 1701, he continually journeyed up and down the Great North Road. He would have eaten 'the cheese of Stilton' during this time and, with Stukeley, considered it as famous as Parmesan. In his three-volume work *A Tour through the Whole Island of Great Britain*, published at intervals from 1724 to 1726, Defoe mentions the town of Stilton on a number of occasions. However, it seems that the 'christening' of Stilton cheese had not taken place when he was visiting the town regularly in the 1690s, as he does not mention it by this name. By way of contrast, he describes Cheddar cheese in great detail, considering it the best in England, if not the world. Considerable varieties of cheese would be on offer in Stilton. This was a seasonal trade, dependent on supply from Midlands farmers, and undoubtedly some types were more palatable than others. It is obvious from the many recorded comments that travellers visiting Stilton expected to be served ripe, mature cheese. Most probably the town had gained a reputation for having such cheese available hundreds of years before Defoe visited the town. Because of the very nature of the product, cheese can be eaten when only a few days old and is equally edible after twelve months if stored correctly; but then, of course, it is totally different in taste and presentation. The travelling public took a liking to the strong mature cheese that was on offer and to meet demand over the year cheese would be placed in store. Some of the early cheeses would have been blue-veined, many would have different coloured mould; even today it is possible to purchase a varied blue-veined cream cheese.

The first published reference to a cheese called Stilton was made in 1722 by William Stukeley, and repeated extensively in *The Country Housewife and Lady's Director, in the Management of a House, and Delights and Profits of a Farm*. This book was compiled by Professor Richard Bradley of the University of Cambridge, and ran to many editions. Stilton cheese is referred to on page 76 of the 1728 edition, with a note that it has been made for some years. The author also comments

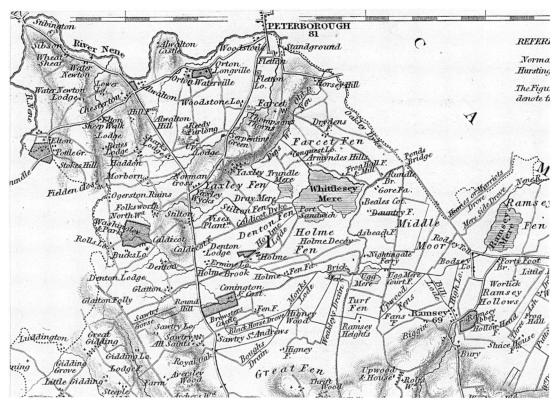

Part of a map published by Chapman & Hall in 1834 showing the area around the town of Stilton. Most of the fen was drained but Dray Mere, Trundle Mere and Whittlesey Mere had yet to be drained and were still a source of seasonal food: ducks.

A romantic illustration of the toll gate at Stilton by Hugh Thomson, c. 1880. The first toll gate was set up at Stilton in 1663 to enable taxes to be levied on the users of the highway. This allowed improvements to the road surface to be made by the local trustees.

on a sample that he purchased from the 'Master of the Blue Bell Inn in Stilton', who supplied his customers with full cheeses to order when in season. From this reference it is obvious that it was a seasonal trade and had not reached the importance it did in later years. During this early part of the eighteenth century, the famous horseman Cooper Thornhill was in charge of The Bell. He entered into a business arrangement with cheese-maker Mrs Frances Pawlett of Wymondham and was undoubtedly the person responsible for establishing the sale of this speciality cheese as an all-the-year-round commodity instead of a recommended cheese obtained seasonally.

This famous innkeeper was born at Leake near Boston in Lincolnshire, possibly in the year 1705, and was baptized there on 16 April 1710. The son of Joseph and Frances Thornhill, he married his first wife Mary in 1730 and purchased The Bell Inn during the same year. They had a number of children together and Mary died in 1752. In 1754 he married Orme Bailey in Stilton parish church; they had no children.

Thornhill was a leading sportsman of his day and in 1745 he took up a wager of 500 guineas to ride 200 miles in less than 15 hours. He duly rode on horseback from Stilton to The Kings Arms, Shoreditch, London, returned to Stilton, then back to Shoreditch – a non-stop journey of 213 miles, which took him twelve hours fifteen minutes. He started on Monday 29 April at 4.00 a.m. and won his wager at 4.15 p.m. This extraordinary feat involved nineteen horses and eighteen changes. A broadsheet poem recording the event was published in 1745 entitled *The Stilton Hero: O Tempora! O Mores.* On another occasion Thornhill arrived at Kimbolton racecourse on his own mare. Watching the main event, he made derogatory remarks about the runners, entered the race without dismounting and won easily, carrying off the prize and trophy.

Thornhill entered into a business arrangement with Frances and William Pawlett to market their Stilton cheese from The Bell Inn in the 1740s; this continued until his death in 1759 at the age of 54. An opportunist, he recognized the uniqueness of Stilton cheese and was responsible for creating the Stilton cheese industry, conveying stage wagon loads to his connections in London. He not only traded in cheese but also in corn, as the east of England representative for the bankers Coutts & Co., throughout the East Midlands, Lincolnshire and East Anglia. Coutts considered him to be 'one of the most considerable corn factors in England'. He purchased the Angel Inn on 30 January 1743 for £850, monopolizing the cheese trade in the town. After his death The Bell was run by A.B. Clark, who passed the business on to his son-in-law, Henry Thornton. In 1776 John Pitts purchased the inn, selling it on 14 June 1796 by auction. Part of the advertisement reads: 'There is also a very considerable Cheese trade attached to the Inn.' It was purchased by John Gibbs who sold it in 1814 to Mrs Scarborough of Buckden, who made her son landlord. These owners and landlords enjoyed a period of prosperity made possible only through the energies of Cooper Thornhill and the skills of Frances Pawlett. Together they had applied standards so that their cheese was truly the 'Famous Stilton Cheese'.

In 1784 John Palmer, the Controller-General of Post, set up the first mail coach run and by 1790 mail coaches were in operation all over Britain. The coach from Edinburgh to London, which stopped at Stilton, covered the journey of 400 miles in a time of two days and three nights, one of the fastest coaches on any route. The mail coaches were sturdily built, carrying six passengers and an armed guard. The great coaching inns came into their own. In Stilton, The Bell, The Angel, The George and The Talbot did tremendous trade. Night and day the coaches kept the townspeople awake. Horses were changed, often the guard and drivers were relieved, but not the passengers, if they had booked a journey from London to Edinburgh. They had time only to snatch a quick meal of cheese, bread and beer, the standard fare at all the hostelries in Stilton.

In July 1635 Charles I commanded that a 'running post' between Edinburgh and London be set up. Stables were built and the first 'pony express' started. A hard-ridden horse will travel about 70 miles before it requires a long rest, and stables at The Blue Bell Inn and other hostelries were enlarged to hold the change of horses. The post boy rested a while, refreshed himself with ale and cheese, and was soon on his way again. This anonymous painting was produced in 1670.

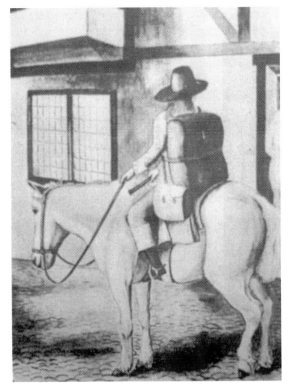

John Blagg, a post boy who carried the mail by stage coach on the Great North Road, is depicted here in an engraving published in 1830. After John Palmer set up the first mail coach run in 1784, the mail was carried in a coach and not by a rider on horseback. Stilton cheese came into its own as the original fast food for coachmen and passengers alike. This was all to end in the 1840s, when the railway system offered a more stable system of transport.

During this era, The Angel Inn emerged as the premier hostelry in the town. It was controlled into the nineteenth century by the formidable Miss Worthington, in later years an upstanding lady who proclaimed that only she offered the true blue-veined Stilton, not the imitation on offer in other inns in the town: 'Her cheese was made in Leicestershire the home of true Stilton Cheese.' The famous coachman C.T.S Birch Richardson, who plied his trade from 1823 to 1875, met this formidable lady in 1823 and related the following story. Two ladies happened to be staying overnight at The Angel Inn and in the morning complained bitterly that their bed had been damp. The indignant Miss Worthington proclaimed that she had never heard of a damp bed in Stilton before, and if it was really so it must have been from the perspiration of the young married couple who had slept in it the night before last. The Angel had facilities for stabling 300 horses with a smithy attached that not only shod horses but cattle on the way to the Smithfield markets. These animals had been rested on Stilton Fen, grazing, to be fattened up for the last part of their journey before slaughter in London.

The golden years of stage coach travel were from the 1790s to the 1840s, and during this period the marketing of Stilton cheese from the town peaked. There must have been hundreds of suppliers, controlled by many middlemen, and legends were established and fortunes made by the lucky Leicestershire farmers, especially in the village of Wymondham, a parish very close to the Great North Road.

The opening of the Midland and the Great Northern railway lines connecting Peterborough with London in the early 1840s saw the beginning of the end of the stage coach business, and the golden years of the Stilton cheese trade also came to an end. The coaching trade continued locally but the long-distance coach trade ceased, as did the wholesale marketing of cheese from Stilton. The Leicestershire farmers marketed their product through wholesalers via the railway system, direct to London. Gradually, because of loss of trade, the fine coaching inns around Stilton fell into disrepair and many of them closed down. Today the four main inns in the town are enjoying a new-found prosperity: The George is now called The Stilton Cheese and The Bell has been restored to its former glory, a monument to one of England's most famous food products, Stilton cheese.

The sign of The Bell, Stilton, 1880.

The famous Miss Worthington offering a traveller a night's lodging at The Angel Inn, Stilton. This landlady proudly displayed a sign outside her hostelry stating that she sold 'Cheese made in Leicestershire the home of true Stilton Cheese'. She ran this inn during the early years of the nineteenth century.

Miss Worthington was the granddaughter of William and Frances Andrews. After William's death, Frances married William Pawlett. It is presumed that Frances Pawlett arranged for the inn to be passed into the hands of her family. The Worthington family lived on Thorne Lane in the village of Wymondham, a short distance from the farmhouse where Frances had lived with her first and second husbands. Worthington House is now situated in the renamed Edmondthorpe Road.

Daniel Defoe (1660–1731): an engraving of a portrait by Van de Gucht. Defoe was an extensive traveller as well as an author and visited the small town of Stilton on many occasions, especially during 1697 to 1701 when he served as a secret agent for William III. One of Defoe's most important works was *A Tour through the Whole Island of Great Britain*, published between 1724 and 1726. In this book he mentions visits to the town of Stilton on five occasions. He was also obviously influenced by other authors, especially William Stukeley.

Cooper Thornhill (1705–59) on horseback: an engraving made in 1745 recording his famous non-stop ride of 213 miles between London and Stilton in April of that year. This print was sold at Cornhill, London, by Thomas Baker. Cooper Thornhill was a Lincolnshire dealer who travelled throughout the Midlands and East Anglia purchasing corn and later Stilton cheese. His prowess as a rough rider was legendary, and enabled him to hunt with the Melton hunts and travel long distances during a working day, buying and dealing in farm produce, which was eventually traded on in London.

With the improvement of the highway by the various turnpike trusts, travel increased along the Great North Road. Between 1780 and 1790, competition for providing refreshment for the coach trade was intense, and many innkeepers distributed specially printed cards showing the two main routes out of London. This card favours the route through Huntingdon, 71¼ miles as opposed to the 74½ miles on the alternative route. Most travellers going north stopped at the town of Stilton. The premier inns were The Angel and The Bell. The Talbot and The Woolpack accommodated the serving class.

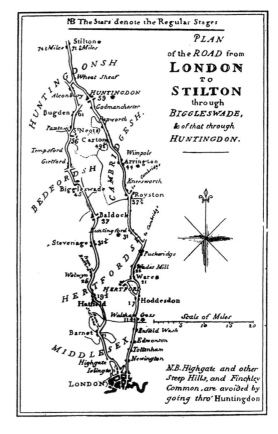

The memorial stone that lies over the tomb of Mary and Cooper Thornhill in the graveyard of St Mary's Church, Stilton. Cooper Thornhill commissioned this carved stone to be placed over his wife's grave when she died in 1752. Thornhill himself died in 1759, and his second wife interred him with Mary.

An early nineteenth-century engraving recording a bare-fist prize fight that took place at Stilton between Richard Humphries and Dan Mendoza on 6 May 1789 in Mr Thornton's Park, in a large tent with a spectators' gallery. The laid-out arena accommodated 3,000 spectators. It was a controversial fight which Mendoza won after twenty-five rounds by using a fine boxing technique. Beer, wine and Stilton cheese were consumed in large quantities.

Filling the boot of a coach in the yard of The Bell Inn, Stilton, *c.* 1840. Among the packages lie a brace of mallard obtained from Stilton Fen and a well-wrapped Stilton cheese, all bound for London. This illustration is after a drawing by Hugh Thomson.

The courtyard of
The Bell Inn,
Stilton, *c.* 1880,
after a drawing by
Herbert Railton.

The Bell at Stilton, in a reproduction of the coloured lithograph by Cecil Aldin, published by Richard Wyman &
Co. Ltd in 1903. This is one of a series of six prints produced by Aldin featuring stage coaches on famous roads.
On this print the inn sign shows a blue bell, the colour used well into the twentieth century; for some unknown
reason, it is now painted red. Until the 1730s this famous inn was always known as The Blue Bell Inn.

A drawing of The Bell Inn, Stilton, 1900, by Charles G. Harper.

Stilton main street, *c.* 1900. On the left is The George Inn, formerly the Woolpack and now The Stilton Cheese. The area to the west of Stilton was a sheep-grazing area, hence the name 'Woolpack'. Before Stilton cheeses were stacked high in the wide road that runs through the town, rolls of fleece were also marketed from this locality, especially during the medieval period. Ewes' milk was also made into a local cream cheese by shepherds' wives.

Main Street, Stilton, looking south, *c.* 1930. A lorry is parked outside The Stilton Cheese Inn. In recent years a considerable number of vaulted tunnels and cellars have been uncovered adjacent to the various inns in the town, used to store the large quantities of cheese while it was maturing.

Main Street, Stilton, looking north, *c.* 1930. In the centre is The Stilton Cheese Inn with a lorry outside. To the right is The Bell Inn and on the left is The Angel Inn, standing at its full height. Today it is much reduced following a disastrous fire. Further down the highway stands The Talbot Inn.

The Bell Inn, Stilton, *c.* 1934. The Bell is considered the premier inn at Stilton, although this was not always the case. The main hostelry retailing cheese during the late eighteenth and early nineteenth centuries was The Angel, on the opposite side of the road. The extensive cellars used in the cheese maturing process still exist under the present building. At the height of the coaching and cheese retailing era, between 1839 and 1845, the town of Stilton boasted fourteen public houses: in High Street The Earl Grey, The Greyhound, The Bird in the Hand, The Angel Hotel, The Goat, The Bell, The Crown (later The Golden Fleece); in Church Street The Wheatsheaf, The Crown; in North Street The George and Dragon, The Talbot, The George; in Fen Street The Boot and Shoe and the Fen Ally beer shop.

The Bell Inn, Stilton, 1957. During the Second World War, this famous inn enjoyed a period of prosperity even though Stilton cheese was unobtainable. Two of the notable guests during this period were the heavyweight boxing champion of the world Joe Louis and the American film star Clark Gable.

Jack Easom, secretary of the Stilton Cheese Makers' Association, standing outside The Bell Inn, Stilton, in 1968, a look of disgust on his face at finding it closed, especially as he had travelled from Melton Mowbray to deliver a complimentary cheese. The Bell was closed for a number of years during the 1960s and '70s.

Richard Landy producing a model of a presentation Stilton stand in his pottery in Stilton, March 2005. See also page 156, where Cooper Thornhill's birth is recorded by this craftsman.

John Stockdale of Webster's Dairy, Saxelbye, starting the traditional Easter Stilton cheese rolling contest, March 1964, the year in which it was revived by the landlords of The Talbot and The Bell. This annual contest takes place on the main street of Stilton. Today it is normally run in May and is organized by the Stilton Community Association.

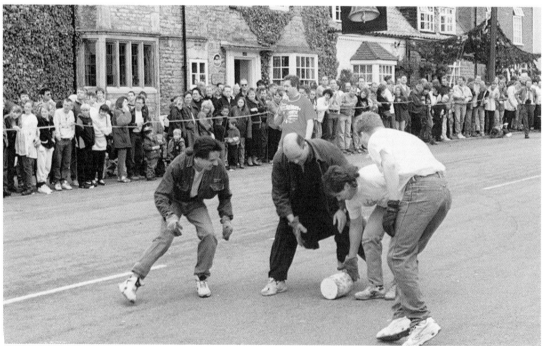

Contestants in the annual Stilton cheese rolling competition in the 'Angel Lane' outside The Bell Inn, Stilton, 8 May 1995. The rules are:

1. *Teams will consist of four members including the captain.*
2. *Teams will be all male or all female.*
3. *No one under the age of 15 years may be included in a team.*
4. *Cheeses must be rolled by hand; no kicking, throwing or picking up of cheeses is allowed and teams must keep to their allotted lanes.*
5. *The first cheese to strike the end boards of the course wins.*
6. *The referee's decision is final.*

3

Melton Mowbray

A s the town of Melton Mowbray is noted for the production of Stilton cheese, it is a remarkable fact that no such cheese was manufactured within its precincts in purpose-built dairies before the end of the nineteenth century. It was the centre of the trade because of its position as a market town. Possibly a market had operated here for more than a thousand years, offering agricultural produce; when surpluses accrued, cheese would be offered for sale and trade. Wholesalers, merchants and cheese factors marketed cheese from the end of the eighteenth century onwards.

The first Stilton Cheese Fair in the town was inaugurated in September 1883 by the Town Estate, and proved a very successful event, with 12,672 Stilton cheeses being sold at prices varying from 10*d* to 1*s* 1½*d* per pound. The market committee decided to repeat the fair in November and, as this was also a great success, it was decided to hold three fairs per year. This continued until the First World War brought a halt to the proceedings. To cater for the fair, the market and adjoining streets were marked out in plots with chalk, similar to a car-park. Farmers brought their cheeses to the market very early in the morning and stacked them on layers of straw. Buyers from London and all the principal cities in Britain would move from batch to batch, boring holes in selected cheeses with a special tool, tasting all that was on offer and then negotiating a price. By the end of the morning all the cheese would be sold, being loaded on railway drays to be conveyed to the two railway stations in the town.

At the end of the nineteenth century, only one specialist dairy was producing and marketing Stilton cheese in the town: Thomas Nuttall's dairy on North Street. Tuxford & Nephews were factoring cheese. Now named Tuxford & Tebbutt, they are today producing cheese in the town, one of the pioneers of the modern Stilton cheese industry. Elizabeth Wood and her son were milking cows and making a seasonal Stilton cheese at their smallholding on King Street in the early 1850s. On 28 October 1854, at the laying of the foundation stone at the Corn Exchange on Nottingham Street, William Thorpe Tuxford (listed in Melville's Leicestershire directory for 1854 as a steam flour miller and Stilton cheese factor, operating in Sherrard Street) made an impassioned speech in support of a change of name for Stilton cheese: 'The finest and most splendid cheese in the world is made within a circuit of ten miles of this place, Melton Mowbray being the centre. The cheese is called Stilton, but from this time I say, call it Meltonian Cream Cheese.' That name did not catch on!

Today Stilton cheese is sold at a number of outlets in the town, and can be purchased direct from the town's only manufacturer Tuxford & Tebbutt, which is situated on Thorpe End. The local tourist office publishes a leaflet detailing a Stilton trail in the town.

An engraving by J. Walker of a drawing by John Throsby, published on 30 January 1790. This is the earliest printed illustration of Stilton cheese. Two farmers are approaching the town of Melton Mowbray along what is now Scalford Road. One is riding a pack-horse with panniers laden with Stilton cheese for sale in the town.

The first Stilton cheese fair, a view of Sherrard Street, September 1883. The entrance to Lamberts Lane is on the right. On this corner stands the shop of Thomas Edward Smith. Further along Sherrard Street on the right stands the Wheatsheaf Tavern, run by the Sharman family; they eventually closed this public house and opened a garage on the site. On the left stands the post office, where George Sanders was postmaster.

A cheese fair in the Market Square, Melton Mowbray, *c.* 1890. These fairs were held three times a year, the last one being held on 18 November 1915. In the centre of this photograph stand Mr and Mrs Gilbert of Great Dalby, who were among the organizers of the fairs. Mrs Mary Musson from Wartnaby stands on the right.

By Order of the Urban District Council.

Melton Mowbray Cheese Fairs

ARE HELD ANNUALLY ON

The Second Thursday in APRIL—April 12th, 1900.

The Fourth Thursday in SEPTEMBER—September 27th, 1900.

The First Thursday in DECEMBER—December 6th, 1900.

A newspaper advertisement for the Stilton cheese fairs that were to be run during 1900.

The Market Place, Melton Mowbray, 1904. The cheese fair is just drawing to a close. Stilton cheeses are being loaded on to horse-drawn railway wagons for conveyance to the town's two stations.

A similar scene in 1912.

Mrs Fisher of Great Dalby at a Melton Mowbray cheese fair, 1910.

SHARMAN & LADBURY

ENGINEERS, AND
AGRICULTURAL IMPLEMENT MANUFACTURERS,
SHERRARD STREET AND CATTLE MARKET,
MELTON MOWBRAY

Field Implements and Barn Machinery of all kinds to suit the district.

REPAIRS of all kinds of Agricultural Machinery.

Iron Fencing, Iron Hurdles, Field Gates, Sheep Netting, Wire Netting, Corrugated Iron Roofing Sheets.

Dairy Appliances & Utensils.

BARREL CHURNS,
BUTTER WORKERS,
MILK REFRIGERATORS,
RAILWAY CANS,
SPECIAL AND IMPROVED STILTON
CHEESE HOOPS.

Washing Machines, Dolly Washers, Steam Washers, Wringers and Mangles

OLD ROLLERS TURNED UP AS NEW.

Well-seasoned NEW ROLLERS prepared by special machinery, fitted and fixed on the Premises

A 1892 advertisement for dairy utensils including the 'improved Stilton cheese hoop'.

The New BRITISH Blue-vein Cheese

"GRANTAMEDE"

In Quality & Flavour surpasses all Imported Products

"BEVAMEDE-STILTON"
(National Mark)

BEVAMEDE DAIRIES LTD.
WICKLOW LODGE
MELTON MOWBRAY

Phone : Melton Mowbray 400

A 1938 advertisement for Bevamede Dairies whose offices and warehouse were situated at the rear of Wicklow Lodge, off Burton Road, Melton Mowbray. The main Stilton-producing dairy was at Wymondham (see p. 68) with two supporting dairies at Hickling Pastures and Nether Broughton.

A cheese fair at Melton Mowbray, *c.* 1910.

A cheese fair at Melton Mowbray, 1912. It is interesting to note the various sizes of Stilton cheeses on offer.

A brass plate soldered to the side of a 'Ladbury' Stilton cheese hoop. This hoop was purchased by Mrs Doris Wright of Ingarsby Lodge in the 1920s, and was used continuously until 1961.

A Stilton cheese hoop made by Alfred Ladbury & Son, 3 High Street, Melton Mowbray. One of the firm's employees Don McGibbon recalls tying up quantities of the hoops with binder twine for delivery by rail to Hartington in Derbyshire. Local deliveries were made in Melton Mowbray to Henry Morris of North Street and Tuxford and Nephews of Thorpe End, and village deliveries were made to Scalford, Saxelbye and John-O-Gaunt.

Albert Edward Grimbley stands in the doorway of his shop at 10 Sherrard Street, 1908. Grimbley's was a brush manufacturer and also sold all types of baskets made from willow, for carrying individual Stilton cheeses by rail. Hundreds were supplied to the Somerby dairy of F.W. Fryer.

The 'Old Dairy', North Street, Melton Mowbray. Built by Thomas Nuttall in the 1880s, it was sold to Henry Morris in about 1900. After Henry Morris's death in 1920, it was purchased by the Melton Dairy Farmers. In 1936 it came into the ownership of Mathew Skailes and was run by Cropwell Bishop Creamery until 1986, when the Stilton cheese production was transferred to Cropwell Bishop. During the interwar years, Mabs Tyers was the dairy manageress, producing excellent Stilton cheese. Many people in the town can remember purchasing from her basins full of cheese curd scrapings at sixpence a bowl for making cheese cake tarts. Pigs were kept in nearby Charlotte Street, fed on the whey. The top floor of the dairy was a meeting room for a local boy scout group and was occasionally used for Saturday night dances, known as the 'Cheese hop' dances.

The three Cantrill sisters at the entrance to the North Street dairy when Henry Morris was the owner, *c.* 1906.

Miss Smith, Stilton cheese-maker at the North Street dairy, *c.* 1898.

Thomas Nuttall's letterhead for 1896. He commenced making Stilton cheese in large quantities in the very first Stilton cheese factory at Beeby in 1875. At the time this letterhead was issued, he was the leading Stilton cheese manufacturer in the world, winning first prize for his Stilton cheeses in London, Amsterdam and New York. Nuttall owned factories at Melton Mowbray, Beeby and Uttoxeter.

Melton Mowbray Fat Stock Show, 1961, when Colston Bassett Dairy won all the trophies. From left to right: Jack Easom, secretary of the Stilton Cheese Makers' Association; John Stockdale, Websters Dairy; Ernie Wagstaff, manager of the Colston Bassett Dairy; Albert Marston, chairman of shareholders, Colston Bassett Dairy.

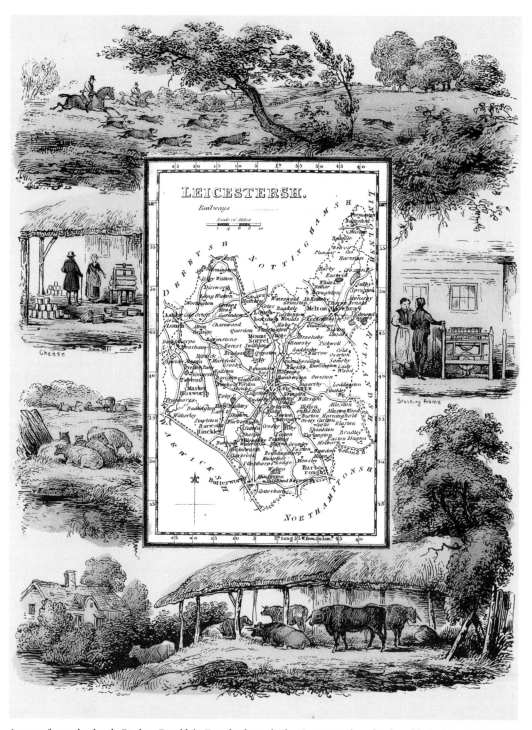

A page from the book *Reuben Ramble's Travels through the Counties of England*, published in 1845. This was a decorated atlas for children containing forty hand-coloured county maps, featuring the main sources of income in each county. The plate for Leicestershire shows fox-hunting, hosiery, cattle, sheep and the manufacture of Stilton and Leicester cheese.

4

The Villages

A t the height of the Stilton cheese trade in the early part of the nineteenth century, there was hardly a farm grazing cows for milk production in Leicestershire, the Lincolnshire wolds, the Vale of Belvoir and parts of Rutland that did not convert its surplus milk to Stilton cheese. It is impossible to list every village where Stilton cheese was made. Like so many products that have a long history, legends develop combined with tradition. A number of villages have been selected here. The premier village is Wymondham, which has a long history of cheese production. As a result of the sixteenth-century enclosures, more farmers manufactured pressed and unpressed cheese, and the probate inventories covering farmers who died with cheese stored in their cheese chambers and dairies are too numerous to list. Two farmers were particularly important: William Whitworth who died in 1618 (see p. 65) and Richard Berriffe who died in 1686, with his probate inventory proved on 6 March. They were both making an unpressed cream cheese that would have been equivalent to a Stilton cheese. In Berriffe's cheese chamber, he had two hasteners (see p. 21), eighteen cheeses, one salt barrel, three cheese boards, and two curd vessels. In his dairy were four pails, one churn, six panchions, nine shelves, one pair of weights and spring, three cheese vats (troughs) and two cheese boards. Some of his farmland was on Crabtree Wong, pasture for grazing cows, near the Stapleford/Wymondham border. The legendary Mrs Pawlett made cheese at Wymondham and it is because of her association with Cooper Thornhill that Stilton cheese gained its place in the history of England.

Many historians have credited Mrs Frances Pawlett as being the inventor of Stilton cheese, a myth that has been perpetuated for more than 200 years since William Marshall's two-volume *Rural Economy of the Midlands Counties* was published in 1790. Mrs Pawlett (née Pick) was certainly involved in the manufacture of Stilton cheese at an early age and it is likely that she standardized the blue-veined cheese that bears the name. What is not certain and can only be surmised is whether Mrs Pawlett considered herself the inventor of modern Stilton cheese. It was first produced in Wymondham, a cheese-making village situated close to the Great North Road. She was taught the art of cheese making by her mother. Frances is believed to have standardized the shape and weight of the cheese, developed the procedure of hand crumbling and packing the curd so that the blue mould formed more quickly, by piercing the maturing cheeses with large needles to speed up this process, and to have called the blue-veined cream cheese, that had been made by various recipes and a variety of people in Wymondham for many centuries, her Stilton cheese, made to her recipe!

The first recorded reference to a cheese called Stilton was made in 1722. Frances Pawlett would have been two years of age. From the wording of the reference, a cheese called Stilton existed before she began her long career as a supreme dairywoman and cheese-maker. Certainly a commercially produced blue-veined cream cheese had been marketed from this parish by generations of farmers' wives.

Frances made excellent blue-veined cream cheeses and her best, together with the best selected from other manufacturers, she called 'My Stilton Cheeses'. Only top quality cheese was delivered to The Bell and The Angel inns at Stilton, to be sold as the famous Stilton cheese. Mrs Pawlett was involved in a substantial marketing of Stilton cheese, delivering wagon-loads of cheeses to Stilton down the Great North Road, and establishing a form of quality control that she maintained for more than forty years. Undoubtedly it was because of her entrepreneurial skills in promoting and selecting only the very best cheese to be retailed at Stilton, that the blue-veined cream cheese became the 'King of Cheeses'.

Frances was born at Sproxton, Leicestershire, in 1720, the second daughter of Richard and Dorothy Pick. Her mother was born in Edmondthorpe, Leicestershire, and was baptized Dorothy Thorne, on 12 April 1689. Richard Pick died in 1752 and his widow died in 1763. Both are buried in Wymondham churchyard. They lived and worked in the parish.

Frances married twice. Her first husband was William Andrews, whom she married at Buckminster on 31 January 1739. They had one child, Richard. Andrews died in 1741 and on 13 October 1742 Frances married William Pawlett, a bachelor of Market Overton, Rutland, in South Witham church, Lincolnshire. They had no children. William was the son of William Pawlett of Market Overton and Mary Adcock of Hambleton, Rutland, and was born in 1712.

It is fairly certain that Frances and William Andrews set up home in the farmhouse on Edmondthorpe Road (at that time called Thorne Lane), Wymondham, which was for many years The Hunters Arms public house. This had been occupied by Frances's great-grandfather, Henry Thorne. They farmed the adjacent land and Frances made a cream cheese with which she established a reputation as a fine dairywoman. On her second marriage, Frances and her new husband continued to live in the farmhouse on Thorne Lane. They never owned any farmland, all their fields being rented and at one time amounting to approximately 169 acres: good pasture, ideal for rearing fine milking cows.

The Pawletts were Rutland farmers, shrewd in business. Perhaps William was aware of Frances's skill as a Stilton cheese-maker and saw the marriage as an ideal partnership in the producing and marketing of large quantities of cheese. As a farmer, it may be presumed that William Pawlett had contact with Cooper Thornhill in his capacity as a corn buyer. Both Pawlett and Thornhill were aware of the potential of cheese sales into London, so they entered into a trading agreement. The Great North Road ran only a few miles to the east of Wymondham and Market Overton, and Frances and her husband William utilized it in their successful business partnership with Cooper Thornhill. In 1743 they were selling him large quantities of cheese for retailing at The Bell and Angel inns at Stilton, transporting it along this important highway with its links to London and Edinburgh.

William Pawlett, as a successful businessman, was involved in civic affairs and served as the village constable for the parish of Wymondham on more than one occasion. He died on 7 October 1787 at the age of 75. Frances continued to run the farm and cheese business for another ten years until 1797, when she gave up most of the farmland to a Mr Parke and vacated the farmhouse to live in a nearby cottage. She witnessed the arrival of the stage coach era in the 1780s and the start of the big boom in the Stilton cheese trade. In June 1806 at the age of 86 she went to live at Little Dalby with her brother's daughter, Frances Pick.

This remarkable woman had developed the Stilton cheese industry with her husband, forming what may have been the first co-operative, collecting fine quality cheese from many farmers in the area, and acting as the wholesale supplier to The Bell, The Angel and possibly other retail outlets in the town of Stilton. More than forty years of trading made her a very wealthy woman, and when she went to live at Little Dalby she wrote her own will, in which her skill as a shrewd businesswoman is very apparent. Frances died on Christmas Eve 1808 and was buried beside her husband William on 28 December. The double slate headstone over the joint graves in Wymondham church-yard carries two short epitaphs: for William – 'a peaceable just man'; for Frances – 'Remember to Die', not a very charitable inscription. Her family were obviously unhappy that they could not get their hands on her money until she was dead, by which time she had outlived her son and most of her close relatives. Susanna Needham, her granddaughter, became the sole beneficiary of her will.

In the following pages a photographic record of a selection of villages is presented. This is not a complete collection, and it is doubtful that a complete collection could ever be made, as in many instances no records exist and no photographs were ever taken. Small factory dairies opened up after 1875 in many villages in the East Midlands; some unsuccessful ones lay even farther afield. In most instances even the building housing the dairy has been demolished.

A Victorian silver-plated scoop, similar to those used for serving Stilton cheese in most of the farmhouse dining rooms of the Stilton cheese-producing area of the East Midlands, until the Second World War.

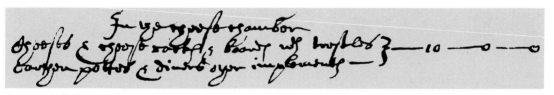

A paragraph from William Whitworth's probate inventory, proved on 2 September 1618 and written in 'secretary hand'. It reads:

In the cheese chamber
    Cheeses & cheese racks a board with trestles }
    Earthern pottes & divers other implements }   10–0–0

He had thirteen 'milch kine' (milking cows) valued at £30. His estate was valued at £655. Whitworth had been a very prosperous farmer who lived in the village of Wymondham and died on 26 August 1618. He is buried in Edmondthorpe churchyard.

Wymondham

The manor house, Wymondham, as illustrated on the estate map drawn in 1652 by S. Partridge for Sir William Sedley. It is probably the birthplace of the blue-veined cream cheese that came to be known as Stilton.

Dorothy Potter (left) and Millie Ecob hanging out the 'cloths' (Stilton cheese strainers) in front of the cheese-maturing buildings, *c*. 1935. Note the ventilation duct on the roof, right.

Barns and storehouse on the site of the manor house owned by the lords of the manor of Wymondham, by the families of Hamelin (*c*. 1150–1290), Berkeley (1290–1635) and Sedley (1635–*c*. 1700). These buildings are shown to the right of the manor house on the plan above. This photograph, taken in 1977, could be of some of the oldest surviving cheese-maturing buildings in England, dating from before 1650.

Remains of the eighteenth-century extension to the Old Manor House, Wymondham, which is incorporated into the present-day factory. Stilton cheese of a very high standard was made here, until restrictions imposed in 1940 stopped production. This placed considerable strain on the company and it eventually went into liquidation, the Wymondham Dairy being sold to William Hill. This enabled his son Peter to extend his business of manufacturing 'Norfolk Stuffing' from locally grown herbs, so ending what was possibly 850 years of cream cheese production on this site. A source of additional income for the Wymondham Dairy was the raising of pigs, fed on whey, for pork pie production.

Three employees of Bevamede Dairies leaning over the wall surrounding the dairy. This 1933 photograph shows the corner of the present-day building that is featured in the photograph above. The seventeenth-century chimney stack has unfortunately been removed. Pictured, left to right, are Nancy Saunders, Miss Swanson and Sarah Wiles, who was manageress of the Wymondham Dairy from 1938 to 1942. Sarah learnt the craft of making fine Stilton cheese at Long Clawson Dairy and is the sister of Tom Wiles, chairman of the Stilton Cheese Makers' Association from 1952 to 1961 and 1968 to 1973.

After the death of Henry Morris in 1920 Wymondham Dairy came into the possession of Bevamede Dairies. They purchased two further Stilton cheese manufacturing dairies at Hickling Pastures (Websters) and Nether Broughton (Greaves). Bevamede Dairies built the factory-style brick extension on to the front of the Old Manor House Dairy at Wymondham in the early 1930s. They over-extended their financial resources, and the extension was never satisfactorily completed because of lack of cash. The main cheese store for the three factories was at Wicklow Lodge, Melton Mowbray.

Stilton cheese-makers at the Bevamede Dairies, Wymondham, 1939. Back row, left to right: Dorothy Mason, Nancy Saunders, Miss Swanson, Dorothy Potter. Front row: Gwen Naylor, Millie Ecob, Vera Huckle, Sarah Wiles.

The Hunters Arms Hotel, Edmondthorpe Road, Wymondham. This had been a farmhouse and the home of Frances Pawlett from 1742 to 1797. She marketed Stilton cheese here. On 9 June 1997 this famous hostelry closed its doors for the last time, and ceased trading as a public house.

The gravestone in Wymondham churchyard of William Pawlett (1712–87) and Frances Pawlett (1720–1808). Frances developed a cheese that had been made in Wymondham for many centuries. With Cooper Thornhill she perfected a formula that was different from the one used by Thornhill's predecessor at the sign of the Bell at Stilton. Her recipe produced a quality cheese, not the inferior variety that was being made in some dairies. The crude recipe that was used to make a cheese of Stilton before the Thornhill/Pawlett era is: Ten gallons of milk and five gallons of cream were mixed; boiling water and after a few minutes a vegetable infusion (rennet) were added. As soon as the curd had settled the whey was run off and the curd was broken up in small lumps, salted and pressed in a vat. The whey was boiled, the pressed curd was placed in the hot liquid for half an hour, then removed and wrapped in linen binders. These were stacked on wooden shelves and turned every day for a month, then stored in a cellar to mature.

An advertising flyer for Stilton cheese, which was distributed from the Wymondham Dairy just after the First World War.

Wymondham Dairy, when it was owned by Henry Morris, *c.* 1910. Left to right: Mrs Bratby, Miss Briggs, Mrs W. Harris, Miss S. Chafer (manageress).

Wymondham Manor House. This building was erected by William Mann in about 1835, as a shrine to Stilton cheese, on land owned by Lord Harborough. William Mann made a fortune from farmhouse Stilton cheeses. Along with the Day family, who possibly made Stilton cheese in the Old Manor House Dairy opposite, he monopolized the Stilton trade from the village after Frances Pawlett retired. John Morris made Stilton cheese in the dairy at this house at the end of the nineteenth century.

Right: A monument to Stilton cheese erected at the expense of Peter Hill on the wall of The Bowery, Wymondham, facing the main road. John (Jack) Morris, a fine Stilton cheese-maker, lived at this house at the turn of the twentieth century. Peter Hill became the eventual owner of the Old Manor House Dairy (Wymondham Dairy), the reputed birthplace of Stilton cheese, in testimony of which he erected this carved stone. *Below:* Advertisement on a speciality wooden box used for conveying Stilton cheese from Wymondham Dairy, *c.* 1930.

Waltham-on-the-Wolds

The staff of Watson's Dairy, Waltham-on-the-Wolds, *c.* 1960. Left to right: -?-, Mary Bestwick, -?-, Flo Woodcock (manageress of the dairy). John Rudkin Morris set up this Stilton cheese-making dairy after the First World War. By 1924 he was producing excellent Stilton. The business was sold to the Watson family in the 1930s, and was run in 1940 by William Watson, jnr. In 1947 a part share was bought by Frank Strickland-Skailes who took over complete control in the early 1960s, closing the business down in 1965.

A. Mathews & Skailes Ltd service van, *c.* 1965, which regularly visited the Waltham-on-the-Wolds dairy. The main offices were at Tooley Street, London, with dairies at Bristol, Midsomer Norton, Langport and Cropwell Bishop, in addition to those making Stilton cheese at North Street, Melton Mowbray, and High Street, Waltham-on-the-Wolds.

Saxelbye

Henry Morris's dairy at Saxelbye in 1920, the year in which he died aged 64. Henry was a leading force in the Stilton cheese trade from the early 1880s until his death, having an interest in at least seven dairies in villages around Melton Mowbray. He expanded into the manufacture of the famous Melton Mowbray pork pie, purchasing Evans and Company in 1910 for £1,300. See pages 60–7 in *The History of the Melton Mowbray Pork Pie*.

98

Monthly Total Stock.

1910		Oct. 12	Nov. 1	Dec. 1							
Oct. 12	Melton	1888									
"	Wymondham	1747									
	Top. Dairy	1866									
	Stathern	2182									
	White Lodge	2072									
	Hames	89									
	Smith's	45									
		9889									

Page 98 from Henry Morris's stock book. On 12 October 1910 he had 9,889 Stilton cheeses in stock at his dairies at Melton Mowbray, North Street; Wymondham, the Old Manor House Dairy; Saxelbye, Top Dairy; Stathern; Eastwell, White Lodge; Wymeswold, Hames; and Smiths.

A SILVER CUP, Value £10 (for Makers only),
given by JOSEPH P. SWAIN, Esq.

Exhibitors competing for the Swain Cup must enter two lots in Class 2, and state on Entry Form "Swain Cup."

The Cup becomes the property of the Exhibitor who first wins three times unless meanwhile it has been won two years in succession.

The winner of each year (until won outright) will be allowed to hold the Cup until fourteen days before the following year's Show, on giving a satisfactory guarantee of its safe custody to the Secretary of the Society.

The following CONDITIONS must be observed :—

The Cup shall be awarded to the finest Stilton (in the opinion of the Judge) in any Class in which Twelve Stiltons or more are exhibited of the season's make in which the Show is held, entered by and being the property of the Maker ; subject to there being six or more Entries in each year.

The Judge's decision in all cases to be final.

Won in 1904 by Mrs. C. Fairbrother, Beeby Leicester.
Won in 1905 by A. P. Oliver, Marefield, Tilton, Leicester.
Won in 1906 by Mrs. C. Fairbrother, Beeby, Leicester.
Won in 1907 by A. P. Oliver, Marefield, Tilton, Leicester.
Won in 1908 by William Cowan, Baggrave, Leicester,
Won in 1909 by Tuxford & Nephews, Melton Mowbray.
Won in 1910 by J. Rigby, South Croxton, Leicester.
Won in 1911 by Belvoir Vale Dairies, Harby, Melton Mowbray.
Won in 1912 by Henry Morris, Saxelbye, Melton Mowbray.
Won in 1913 by Mrs. Frith, Lowesby, Leicester.
Won in 1914 by Henry Morris, Saxelbye, Melton Mowbray.

N.B.—Four Competitors in each Class, or Second Prize withheld unless great merit. No exhibitor will be allowed to take more than one Prize in a Class. Cheese not to be ironed previous to Competition.

Entrance Fees—Classes 1 and 2, Members 2/6 each entry ; Non-Members 5/-.

The bottom half of the 1915 entry form submitting twelve Stilton cheeses for the Leicestershire Agricultural Society 1904 Challenge Cup. This was presented by Joseph Paddy Swain, to be awarded annually at the Leicestershire Agricultural Show. In 1915 the cup was won by The Scalford Dairy Ltd, and in 1916 by Henry Morris, Manor Farm, Saxelbye, for the third time. This meant that he retained the cup, and it has remained in the possession of the Morris family ever since.

The Swain Cup, won outright by Henry Morris in 1916. Henry was born on 13 November 1853 and died on 17 August 1920.

Mrs Winifred (Wagstaff) Beard, who was manageress of Saxelbye Dairy in 1919 when it won two first prizes at the London Dairy Show and a gold medal at the Cardiff Royal Show.

Nether Broughton

Staff, Thompson's Dairy, 1918. Back row, left to right: Mrs Harvey, Dorothy Marriott, Florrie Lovett, Hetty Randall. Front row: Rose Williamson, Margaret Rouse, Eva Taylor. When this photograph was taken Dorothy Marriott was fourteen, on a Stilton cheese-making course at Thompson's Dairy. After a short time she left to run her father's farmhouse dairy at Broughton Lodge, making one or two Stiltons a day during the season (April to November). There were two Stilton cheese-making dairies at Nether Broughton, Thompson's on the Nottingham Road and Greaves on Dairy Lane. The Nottingham Road dairy was a subsidiary of Henry Thompson and Sons Ltd, Food Specialists. The Greaves dairy was a large family-run farmhouse dairy which was sold to Bevamede Dairies in the 1930s. Both of these dairies closed at the outbreak of the Second World War.

A sign that was displayed at the junction of Dairy Lane and the Nottingham to Melton Mowbray road until 1940, when Bevamede Dairies (Greaves) closed. The dairy building still stands on Dairy Lane and has been converted into a row of three terraced bungalows.

Belvoir

Fullarton's engraving of Belvoir Castle in 1834, with the cheese dairies in front.

The Dairies, Belvoir Castle, *c.* 1905. A Mrs Stilton made Stilton cheese in these dairies in about 1800.

Beeby

The Quorn Hunt outside the Manor House, Beeby, 1890s. This was the main office of Stilton cheese-maker Thomas Nuttall (see p. 61). Thomas Nuttall opened the first Stilton cheese factory in 1875 at the age of 40. This factory stands behind the trees to the right of the photograph.

Four pyramids of Stilton cheese made and exhibited by Thomas Nuttall of Beeby at the Islington Dairy Show, 1877. He won first prize and medal for the best British blue-veined cream cheese. This was possibly the largest-ever display of Stilton cheese at any exhibition anywhere in the world.

At the Islington Dairy Show held on 8 October 1878, Thomas Nuttall of Beeby built a replica of Cleopatra's Needle from Stilton cheese. For this exhibit he was awarded the gold medal for the best blue-veined cream cheese, a silver medal and a special silver cup for an outstanding display. Queen Victoria was so impressed when she visited this cheese fair that she promptly purchased all of the cheeses that were used to build this amazing display.

Thomas Nuttall's stand at the London Dairy Show, 1881, for which he was awarded first prize. 1881 was the year in which he opened his shop, selling farm produce in Newgate Street, London.

Thomas Nuttall (1835–1926), the founder of the first factory producing Stilton cheeses. He took over a disused Leicester cheese factory at the Manor House, Beeby, near Leicester, in 1875 and adapted it to produce factory-made Stilton cheese. He employed thirty people and purchased milk from farmers in the surrounding villages. Before 1875, all Stilton cheese was made in farmhouse dairies from the farm's own milk and was still a seasonal product. Thomas Nuttall changed the industry for ever. He soon had his competitors, many local farmers deciding they could convert their milk to Stilton cheese rather than sell it to him. Nuttall built a dairy at Melton Mowbray to centralize his supply, although there were still supply problems and family differences. His son, John, commenced running the Hartington Dairy, producing Stilton cheese in Derbyshire.

Thomas and Louisa Nuttall's grave in Beeby churchyard.

Lodge Farm, Little Beeby, *c.* 1925. This was the home of Charlotte Fairbrother until 1902, when she purchased Grace Cup Farm, Beeby. Mrs Fairbrother was a champion Stilton cheese-maker, winning many trophies locally and in London.

Charlotte Fairbrother in 1906 with the cups she had won for her Stilton cheeses. Left to right: British Dairy Farmers' Association 1890, British Dairy Farmers' Association 1892, The Leicestershire Agricultural Society, Swain Cup 1906, -?-, British Dairy Farmers' Association 1897, along with seven silver and three bronze medals.

Allexton

Allexton Lodge Farm, Allexton, near Uppingham, *c.* 1935. From 1929 to 1935 Mr and Mrs A. Staples made prize-winning Stilton cheese in the dairy attached to this farm, as they had also at Lodge Farm, Beeby, which they farmed from 1904 to 1929.

Mrs A. Staples, 1930s.

The certificate awarded with the Simkin & James Challenge Cup, which was won in 1929, 1930 and 1933 by Mrs Staples of Allexton Lodge. On winning the trophy three times, the successful exhibitors were allowed to keep the cup. It is still in the possession of the family.

Kirby Bellars

As early as 1360, the monks of Kirby Bellars Priory would have made cream cheese from cows' and ewes' milk, in which blue veining may have formed as it matured.

Colonel Francis Hacker of Colston Bassett, who occupied the manor house at Kirby Bellars during the Civil War. Through his endeavours, cheese from this house was distributed to Cromwell's troops.

The Quorn Hunt at Kirby Bellars mansion house, *c.* 1905. The building at the rear of the house was possibly the dairy used by Mary, the daughter of Sir Erasmus de la Fontaine.

Remains of one of the 'enclosing' walls possibly built by the monks at Kirby Bellars Priory during the fourteenth century. These very early enclosures enabled cattle to be grazed, thus increasing milk yields. Part of the manor house holding is now Park Farm.

Kirby Bellars' seventeenth-century manor house contains part of the remains of the Augustinian priory where a cheese, the forerunner of the modern-day Stilton cheese, was developed.

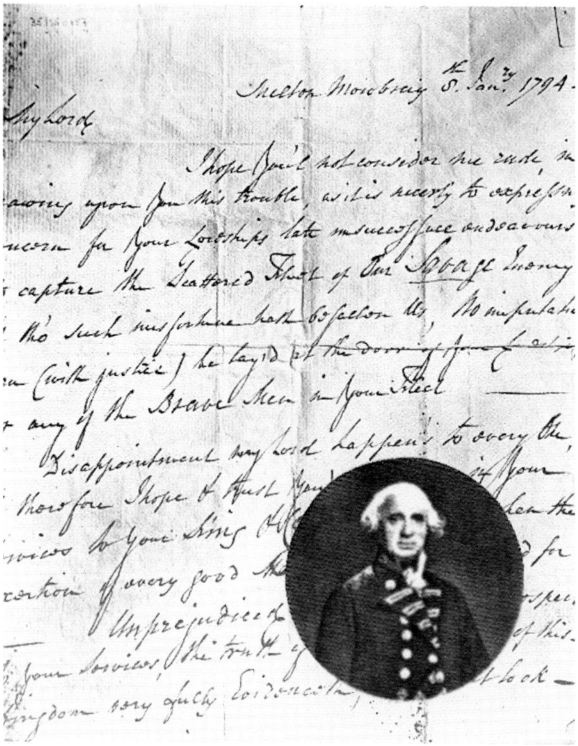

An extract from a letter written in 1794 to Admiral Lord Howe of Langar, with his portrait.

A typewritten copy of the letter illustrated above. The 'Original Dairy House' can only be Kirby Bellars Priory. It is interesting to note that parts of the Vale of Belvoir had still to be enclosed.

TO : ADMIRAL LORD HOWE

Melton Mowbray, 5th January 1794

My Lord,

I hope you'll not consider me rude in drawing upon you this trouble, as it is merely to express my concern for your Lordship's late unsuccessful endeavours to capture the scattered Fleet of our Savage Enemy's; and tho' such misfortune hath befallen us, no implications can (with justice) be lay'd at the door of your Lordship or any of the brave men in your Fleet.

Disappointment, my Lord, happens to every One, and therefore I hope and trust you'll not relax in your services to your King and Country at a time when the exertion of every good man is required and wished for.

Unprejudiced minds who have retrospect on your services, the truth of which the history of this Kingdom very fully evidenceth, cannot but look upon your Lordship with the same esteem as I confess I bear to you. And as a token of that respect I have done myself the pleasure of sending your Lordship a Stilton Cheese made at the Original Dairy House about 3 miles from this place. And of which I beg the Honour of your Lordship's acceptance. I am my Lord, with sincere wishes for your Health and future success, Your Lordship's dutiful

& obedient servant

Edw. E. Stokes

If you can spare your knife from the cheese a couple of months, it will be more ripe and pleasant to your palate than at the present. I am sorry to inform your Lordship that the Commissioners for Stathern Inclosure have not yet settled their Award owing to their multiplicity of business. Hope a meeting will be soon appointed for that purpose.

Laund

Laund Abbey, 1800. Early in the sixteenth century, cheese that had been made in the estate's dairies from ewes' milk was being sold on Stamford market.

Sheep grazing in front of Laund Abbey, as they have done for centuries. The grounds and the immediate estate have never been enclosed. This is sheep-grazing country, producing, during the medieval period, large quantities of seasonal cheese made from ewes' milk. It was not until the eighteenth century, when some outlying farms owned by the estate had been enclosed, that sufficient quantities of cows' milk became available to make a seasonal cheese.

Somerby

The Grange Farm, Somerby, *c*. 1930. This was built in 1890 by Brasenose College, Oxford, which owned the land. Violet Louise Fryer stands in the doorway. Stilton cheese was made from about 1920 until 1935 at this farmhouse, at which time Frank Fryer decided that he could get a better return for his milk by selling direct to John-O-Gaunt dairy.

Francis William (Frank) Fryer helping his daughter Mary to mount a pony, 1933. The Grange Farm Dairy is in the background. The chimney directly behind the pony's head indicates the position of the outside copper that heated the water used in Stilton cheese manufacture.

Station—John o' Gaunt. L.N.E.R. & L.M.S. Joint.
Telegrams—Somerby, Melton Mowbray.
Phone—Somerby 6.

M The Bursar, Brasenose College, Oxford.

Memo from **F. W. FRYER,**

STILTON CHEESE MAKER AND FARMER

SOMERBY, MELTON MOWBRAY.

Grange Farm was owned by Brasenose College, Oxford, which supported the production of Stilton cheese. A list was forwarded to the farm every Christmas for quantities of Stilton cheese to be sent out to the many people who were connected with the college. Wicker baskets were supplied by Grimbleys of Melton Mowbray (see p. 59) to hold the individual cheeses, which were distributed via John-O-Gaunt railway station. This photograph shows the label that was tied to the lid of the basket, with a copy of a bill head invoicing the bursar.

Frank Fryer, 1940.

A hastener, last used by Frank Fryer in 1935. The 'Brasenose Stiltons' were stacked on these shelves to drain off the whey, which was caught in a bowl under the centre of the bottom shelf (see p. 21). Grange Farm had a 'cheese room', a 'dairy-hastener room' and a cellar where the cheese matured.

One of the original 'leads' used by Frank Fryer. These lead draining troughs were eventually discarded, as troughs made of slate proved more efficient.

A sign board that was displayed on the road that ran adjacent to Grange Farm. The Fryers made approximately four Stilton cheeses per day during the season April to November, from their own milk. The bulk of their production was sold to Brasenose College, Oxford. Surplus cheese was offered locally, and sold direct to retailers and on the local market. Competition from the major producers, who cut prices, was one of the contributing factors that ensured Frank Fryer made his last Stilton cheese in November 1935.

Wartnaby

Church Farm, Wartnaby, *c.* 1920. This was the home of the Musson family who had a long tradition of Stilton cheese manufacture, through the nineteenth and into the early twentieth century.

Mrs Mary Eliza Musson (1844–1922). In 1900 the author Sir Henry Rider Haggard visited Mrs Musson at Wartnaby to discuss the manufacture of Stilton cheese with her, and in his book *Rural England* he quotes her as making the following remark on the manufacture of Stilton cheese: 'that with the exception that they made no noise, they were more trouble than babies'. This is a photograph taken at about that time.

Withcote

Withcote Hall, an engraving from a drawing by J. Pridden, 1793. This hall had a long association with cheese production.

Withcote Lodge, the home of the Pick family who farmed in the village for many generations. Mary Pick, who originated in Great Dalby, was the wife of William Pick, and she died in this house in 1800. Mary produced a fine Stilton cheese to her own recipe, and received much credit for this cheese in the national press and trade publications after her death.

Plungar

W. and J.W. Miller's farmhouse, Plungar, 1920. This farm supported four cheese rooms and a dairy producing considerable quantities of Stilton cheese. Plungar was a centre for Stilton cheese production, with three farmhouses producing cheese from their own milk.

An advertisement for Lot 47 from the catalogue of the sale of part of the Belvoir estate, 1920.

A   Compact   Grass   Holding

situate in the centre of the Village of PLUNGAR, together with the

Farm House and Buildings

containing an Area of

30a.   2r.   9p.

or thereabouts, as follows :—

SCHEDULE.

ORDNANCE No.	DESCRIPTION.	AREA. A.	R.	P.
113	Pasture	2	3	9
121	Do.	10	3	11
115	Do.	3	3	2
116	Do.	1	3	1
117	Do.	6	0	31
75	Do.	3	0	3
76	Do.	1	1	4
111	House, Garden, Paddock and Buildings		2	11
Pt. 112	.. ..		1	17
	TOTAL .. A.	30	2	9

THE RESIDENCE is partly Brick and partly Stone, and Tiled, and contains Kitchen, two Living Rooms, Dairy and Pantry, Cheese Room, four Bedrooms, Attic and usual Out-offices. There is another Range of one large and two small Cheese Rooms.

THE BUILDINGS comprise Nag Stable and Coal Place, and in Field No. 113 is a Stone and Tiled Shed.

There is a Right of Way for all purposes to Fields Nos. 76, 75 and 117 over Field No. 114, in the occupation of Mrs. S. Smith ; also over the adjoining Land on the North-east and North-west to Nos. 75 and 117.

Tenants—Messrs. W. and J. W. Miller.

Little Dalby

Little Dalby Hall, in an engraving from a drawing by J. Pridden, 1794. The village of Little Dalby and its hall gained a reputation as a Stilton cheese-making area during the eighteenth century, principally because of Mrs Elizabeth Orton (née Scarborough) who learnt the craft of cheese-making at Quenby Hall. The Ortons had lived in and around Little Dalby since the thirteenth century, mainly as farmers, and undoubtedly made seasonal cheese from ewes' milk, latterly using surplus cows' milk when the seventeenth- and eighteenth-century enclosures took effect. Frances Pawlett died at Little Dalby in 1808, having lived in the village with her niece Frances Taylor, née Pick, for the last two years of her life. This confused local historians of the time, who often erroneously stated that she was a relative of Mrs Orton.

A photograph of Little Dalby Hall that was used as a postcard, 1904. It was posted in May with a message that the sender was about to start making Stilton cheese.

Harby

Starbuck House, 1922. This was the home of the Starbuck family who made farmhouse Stilton cheese from the middle of the nineteenth century until the First World War. The dairy was in the centre of the house, and the hastener and maturing room were to the left of the building. Mary Jane Starbuck stands behind the gate with her niece Betty in front.

Left: The cover from the prospectus for the 1891 Harby Horticultural Society Show.

✦ DIVISION D. ✦
—— :o: ——
Three Prizes given in each when Twelve compete.
—— :o: ——

FARMERS & SHOPKEEPERS IN FOUR MILES RADIUS.

					Entrance d.
99	Honey 2-lb.	...	...	...	6
100	Best sheaf barley	...	...	...	6
101	Best sheaf oats	...	...	...	6
102	Best sheaf wheat	...	...	...	6
103	Six field turnips	...	...	...	6
104	Six swede turnips	...	...	...	6
105	Six field red carrots	...	...	...	6
106	Six mangolds, red	...	...	...	6
107	Six mangolds, yellow globe	...	...	...	6
108	Twelve best potatoes	...	...	...	6
109	A Cheese	...	...	...	6
110	Butter, 2-lb rolls	...	...	...	6

POULTRY.

111	Best cock	...	...	...	6
112	Best two hens	...	...	...	6
113	Best two ducks	...	...	...	6
114	Best turkey ...	...	...	...	6
115	*Cucumbers*	...	...	...	6

Right: The rules for entering class D of the 1891 show. 'A Cheese' meant one Stilton cheese. Jane Starbuck entered a Stilton cheese for this show and won a prize.

Jane Starbuck (1828–1914), Stilton cheese-maker of Harby, 1890.

Mary Jane Starbuck (1858–1944), Stilton cheese-maker, the daughter of Jane, 1900. The Starbucks made one Stilton per day during the months of April to October.

George Baguley, dealer, farmer and Stilton cheese-maker, standing outside his cottage on the junction with Watson's Lane and School Lane, Harby, 1876. It was on this site that Emberlins started the cheese-making enterprise that became United Dairies and eventually St Ivel.

An Emberlin and Co. Ltd lorry, used for conveying Stilton cheese and other goods, seen on the day it was collected outside J.E. Baines's offices. This vehicle was built and supplied by John Edward Baines, 16 Mill Street, Oakham, Rutland. It was a 25 hp Whitney Denby 30½ cwt truck, registered in June 1916.

The staff of United Dairies, Stilton cheese-makers, Harby, from 1925 to 1929. Back row, left to right: Rose Moulds, Olive Miller, Connie Dickman, Winifred Kirk, Phyllis Dickman, Arthur Adams. Front row: Sally Cumberland, Betty Starbuck, Meg Pickard, 'Nigger' Watson, Alice Coy.

DATE	SOLD TO	No. of Stiltons	Weight lbs.	Price per lb.	Packing and Carriage s. d.	CREDIT £ s. d.
Dec 19	Mosford	2	31½	2/10		4. 9. 3
	J. Gell	1	16	2/10		2. 5. 4
	Green, Barkstone	1	15	2/10		2. 2. 6
	Manor Farm Dairy	6	100	2/10		14. 3. 4
	1 Case					1. 0. 0
	Coleman	6	97	2/10		13. 14. 10
	Spurway	12	186	2/10		26. 7. 0
	12 hamper carr 17/1					2. 13. 1
	J Goodson nott.	2	34	2/10		4. 16. 4
	Carr					1. 0
	Servenus Ltd.	2	33	2/10		4. 13. 6
	Harrop	1	16½	2/10		2. 6. 9
	Carr					6
	J Machin	1	16	2/10		2. 5. 4
	Carr					6
	Sumner Richardson	1	16	2/10	6	2. 5. 10
	Webster	2	31	2/10		4. 7. 10
	Shipman Plunger	2	34	2/10		4. 16. 4
20	Miller	1	15	2/4		1. 15. 0
	Cole. Bottesford	2	34	2/9		4. 13. 6
	2 hampers					6. 0
	Manor Farm Dairy	1	17	2/10		2. 8. 2
	1 hamper					3. 0

The Harby Dairy ledger for 19 and 20 December 1919, showing that Stilton was sold at 2*s* 10*d* per pound. Emberlins and Co. Ltd started business as Stilton cheese-makers in 1911, operating as Belvoir Vale Dairies. They were bought out by Wiltshire United Dairies, *c.* 1920. United Dairies was purchased by Cow and Gate in 1960, eventually becoming Unigate, part of the St Ivel operation.

In 1918 twelve farmers, Messrs Fairbrother, Wilford, Rawlinson, J. Swingler, S. Swingler, Lamin, Heyward, Gale, Stroud, Firmage, Dewey and White formed a cooperative and started Harby Farmers Dairy, producing Stilton cheese. Its creamery closed in 1940. After the Second World War it opened for a short while, but was not successful. The building is now part of the Long Clawson Dairy operation.

Demolition of the original dairy in 1975. This building had been incorporated into the modern structure that was now surplus to requirements. A new factory built on Colston Lane had now commenced producing Stilton. By 1903 the village of Harby had become a centre for Stilton cheese manufacture, with Furmidge and Kemp, William Green, Mary Jane Starbuck and Ybele Gerard Veen all listed as specialist Stilton cheese-makers. In addition, there were farmers such as the Baguleys who were making Stilton cheeses from their surplus milk.

Packing Stilton cheese in wooden boxes to be carried from the storage/maturing cellars, 1927. Left to right: Mr Wills, John Stokes, Arthur Adams, Phyllis Dickman, William Kirk, Betty Starbuck, Connie Dickman.

Harby Dairy, 1927.
Ladling the curd
from the 'leads'. Left
to right (foreground):
Olive Brown, Connie
Dickman, Phyllis
Dickman.

Ladling curd from ceramic sinks, 1950. Left to right: Doris Dyson, Victoria Manchester.

Tom Dunn salting the curd, 1970.

Mick Hemsley and Frank Osborne filling
the hoops (moulds) with curd, 1970.

Frank Osborne turning the hoops in the hastening room, 1970.

Kath Edward and Beat Richards smoothing the coat, 1950. Until the Second World War, scrapings obtained in the rubbing process were sold as a delicacy, much appreciated by people in the Vale of Belvoir.

By the early 1970s the Watson Lane Dairy had outgrown its premises. St Ivel backed Robert Watson's ideas for a purpose-built factory on a greenfield site. Plans were drawn and passed, the site was chosen and work commenced in 1974. Robert invited all the dairy workers to bring their own spades for a united turf-cutting ceremony. Back row, left to right: Janet Muxloe, Ian Clayton, Tom Dunn, Isobel Daw. Front row: Betty Moulds, May Whittle, Muriel Brown, Geoff Furmidge, -?-, Kay Booth, Elsie Emminson, Ruth Booth, -?-, -?-, Jack Allington, Doris Dyson, Hilda Steibjon, Kath Edwards, Joan Watson, Ursula ?, Robert Watson, Irene Brown, Pauline Bowcock, -?-, -?- .

The Harby Dairy being built on Colston Lane, Harby, 1974. Graham Dow and Robert Watson are viewing the work. The Watson family had been involved with this dairy business since 1916 when Herbert Watson became manager of Emberlins; his wife Mabel was also a supreme cheese-maker. In 1954 Herbert retired and his son Robert took over. He had inherited all his mother's skills as a brilliant Stilton cheese-maker. In 1976 Robert parted company with the dairy, bringing to an end sixty years of Watsons making fine Stilton cheese in Harby.

The maturing room at the St Ivel Dairy, Colston Lane, Harby, *c.* 1980. Heather Yates, in the foreground, is turning Stilton cheese, with Betty Moulds and Sylvia Chambers in the background.

Millway when part of the Dairy Crest group. In 1988 Millway Foods was formed following a management buyout of the St Ivel Unigate Dairy at Harby. In 1990 the company was bought by Bongrain, a French-based international food company specializing in dairy products. This company sold the cheese-making dairy to Dairy Crest Ltd in 1999, who closed the factory in the spring of 2001 and transferred the production of cheese to Hartington.

Stathern

Stathern Dairy, possibly in 1896. Julia Clarke (who 'married' Henry Morris) is cleaning a hoop, and stands next to Ybele Gerard Veen, a Dutch cheese-maker who assisted Henry Morris as a partner for one year when he started the Stathern Dairy. Veen then set up in business himself as a cheese factor. By 1898, he was making Stilton cheese in his own dairy at Harby; see the invoice heading below.

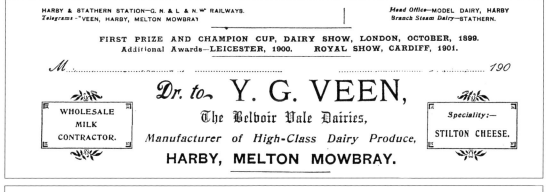

HARBY & STATHERN STATION—G. N. & L & N. W. RAILWAYS.
Telegrams—"VEEN, HARBY, MELTON MOWBRAY"

Head Office—MODEL DAIRY, HARBY
Branch Steam Dairy—STATHERN.

FIRST PRIZE AND CHAMPION CUP, DAIRY SHOW, LONDON, OCTOBER, 1899.
Additional Awards—LEICESTER, 1900.   ROYAL SHOW, CARDIFF, 1901.

M 190

WHOLESALE
MILK
CONTRACTOR.

Dr. to **Y. G. VEEN,**
The Belvoir Vale Dairies,
Manufacturer of High-Class Dairy Produce,
HARBY, MELTON MOWBRAY.

Speciality:—
STILTON CHEESE.

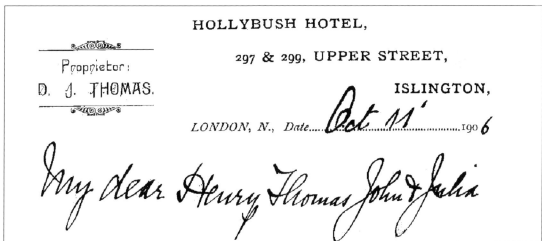

HOLLYBUSH HOTEL,

Proprietor:
D. J. THOMAS.

297 & 299, UPPER STREET,

ISLINGTON,

LONDON, N., Date Oct 11' 190 6

My dear Henry Thomas John & Julia

Letterhead from the hotel at Islington where all the Stilton cheese-makers congregated while exhibiting at the dairy show before the First World War. It comes from a letter sent by Henry Morris to his four children.

The staff of Henry Morris's Stathern Dairy, possibly 1897. Back row, left to right: Charles Denis, Mrs S. Shuttlewood, Mary Elizabeth Brothwell, Mary ?. Front row: -?-, -?-. Mary Brothwell became manageress of Henry Morris's Wymondham Dairy, on the junction of Main Street and Edmondthorpe Road. She married William Ward and died in October 1961 aged 79. Mary was buried in Wymondham churchyard, where she joined many other fine Stilton cheese-makers.

Miss Hemsley, manageress of Stathern Dairy, 1921. This dairy closed in 1940.

Henry Morris with his family, 1912. He went to live at Stathern with his 'wife' Julia in around 1900. Left to right: Henry, jnr, Thomas, Julia, jnr, Julia, John.

Marefield

Snows Farm, Marefield, 1914. Back row, left to right: Arthur Potter Oliver, Elizabeth Oliver (née Leadbetter), Mary Alice Oliver, 'The Twins'. Front row: Arthur George Oliver, William Palmer Oliver, -?-. Arthur Potter Oliver won the Swain Cup at the Leicester Agricultural Show for twelve Stiltons in 1905 and 1907.

Snows Farm, Marefield, the home of the Oliver family for many years, 1907. The Olivers were tenant farmers, on land owned by Captain Hincks, who built the ground-floor extension to the right of the building. This extension was used by Arthur Potter Oliver for making his prize-winning Stilton cheese (see entry form on p. 74).

Wymeswold

Wymeswold, Dairy Crest Dairy, London Lane, *c.* 1985. This building originally built as a primitive Methodist chapel, has now been demolished; an old people's home has replaced it. The village of Wymeswold has a long tradition of Stilton cheese production. In the early part of the twentieth century it supported six Stilton cheese dairies. The earliest was the cheese-making dairy of Samuel Daft, who was well established by 1899, making Stilton on Church Street. At the onset of the First World War three other dairies were producing Stilton cheese: Samuel Hames, Church Street (with Henry Morris); John James, Brook Street; and Emberlin & Co. Ltd, London Lane. After the war, Bill Taylor made Stilton cheese on Clay Street. The dairy shown in this photograph was built by Emberlin & Co. Ltd, and later purchased by J.M. Nuttall's of Hartington in Derbyshire. This was the largest dairy, though still only producing approximately fifty Stiltons per day. Most of the other dairies produced one or two Stiltons per day during the season, obtaining the milk from cows that were 'tented' (tethered) along the very wide grass verges that border the highway around Wymeswold, which to this day are still common land.

J.M.NUTTALL & Co.Ltd

SPECIALISTS IN

ALSO AT
WYMESWOLD, LEICS

WEST DERBYSHIRE FOOD PRODUCTS.

TELEGRAMS:
"NUTTALL, HARTINGTON."

REGISTERED OFFICE:
6 PARK SQUARE, LEEDS,1.

PRIME STILTON, DERBYSHIRE & LEICESTERSHIRE CHEESES.

TELEPHONE:
HARTINGTON 231

DOVE DAIRY,
HARTINGTON
NR. BUXTON.

Letterhead used by the London Lane Dairy at Wymeswold during the 1960s.

Staff from the London Lane Dairy, Wymeswold, with the cup that was won for the best blue-veined cheese at the Leicester Show in 1940. Back row, left to right: Miss I. Baines, Miss McNair (manager, holding the cup), Miss S. Small. Front row: Miss Sampy, Miss Chambers. Miss McNair's brother William was manager of Long Clawson Dairy, and during the Second World War he was chairman of the Stilton Cheese Makers' Association.

Rubbing up Stiltons at the Dairy Crest Dairy at Wymeswold, 1980. Left to right: Peter Hubbard, Ron Crust.

Rubbing up Stiltons at the Dairy Crest Dairy at Wymeswold in 1980. Left to right: Martin Moir, Elsie Hubbard.

The farewell party held at the White Horse public house at Wymeswold. Richard Davies of J.M. Nuttall's organized this event as a 'thank you' gesture for all the employees at the London Lane Dairy, when it closed in 1987. Back row, left to right: Peter Hubbard, David Morris. Front row: Martin Moir, Jean Parry, Ron Riley, Ron Crust (missing, Nancy Kirk). This was the complete workforce when the dairy closed.

Scalford

Scalford Dairy Ltd, 1910. This was formed as a farmers' co-operative in about 1902, and by 1904 it was well established. The manageress was Miss Margaret Rouse. Here the linen draining cloths, bits and binders are being hung in the paddock on clothes lines, drying in the wind.

In 1949 Joe Brindley purchased the Scalford Dairy on behalf of J.M. Nuttall of Hartington. During the Second World War the manufacture of Stilton cheese was not allowed. An attempt to make Red Leicester was not successful, so Scalford closed for the duration of the war. After hostilities ceased, attempts were made to get production under way again, and financial backing was needed – hence the sale to Nuttalls. In 1962 the dairy was purchased by the Milk Marketing Board and became a part of Dairy Crest Food in 1982. On 30 April 1996, this fine old creamery produced its last Stilton cheese; such a small unit (producing only ninety cheeses per day) was no longer viable.

Scalford Dairy always made good Stilton cheese. During the interwar years special deliveries were made direct to the House of Commons, transported by rail from the village station. The manageress in 1916 was Miss Esther Bramley, in 1925 Mrs Elizabeth Allen, and the manager in the 1930s to the mid-1940s was Mr G.M. Kirk. Under new ownership and the direction of William McNair, the dairy soon began winning trophies for its superb Stiltons. Here are the staff of the dairy with the trophies it won in 1959. Left to right: Len Hewitt, Charlie Hill, Reg Logan, Janet Knapp, Phyllis Watchorn, Edna Hewitt. Len Hewitt became manager in 1951.

Len Hewitt stirring in the rennet, 1980. All dairies make slightly different Stilton cheeses. The connoisseur of Stilton can identify cheese made at each of the six producing dairies. Rennet plays an important part. Len retired in 1984; the dairy was then run by John Lambert.

Sutton Bonington

Kingston College, Midland Agricultural and Dairy College Dairy Department, *c.* 1895.

Agriculture in Britain towards the end of the nineteenth century encountered a period of depression, mainly due to overseas competition. Education was seen as one way of improving the quality of locally produced cheese and butter. Funding was obtained via the recently formed county councils. The first courses were travelling dairy schools, well attended, but too short.

The combined county councils of Leicestershire, Nottinghamshire, Derbyshire and the Lindsey Division of Lincolnshire agreed to fund an educational establishment. Lord Belper of Kingston-on-Soar offered to lease his home farm of 160 acres, with buildings, to form Kingston College.

The grand opening of the Midland Dairy Institute at Sutton Bonington took place on Tuesday 17 September 1895. It was performed by the Duke of Devonshire and attended by some 1,000 people.

Of the many courses on offer at Kingston College, the cheese-making courses proved to be most popular. It was possible to attend to learn the finer points of Stilton cheese manufacture, with short courses of six weeks, certificate courses of one year and a diploma course of two years. Dormitory and hostel facilities were provided.

In 1905 the name was changed to the Midland Agricultural and Dairy College, being further consolidated with the Department of Agriculture at University College Nottingham. The year 1915 saw the expansion into Lodge Farm at Sutton Bonington, enabling an administration block and lecture theatre to be built. The hostel facilities were also increased. Then the First World War intervened, and the new buildings became a prisoner-of-war camp for German officers.

In 1924 the contributing counties included Rutland. The new buildings were finally opened for their intended use in 1928. The Dairy Department moved in immediately and the Kingston site was relinquished.

From the early 1920s until 1939 expansion of courses took place. In 1935 there were 112 students attending a variety of courses: 55 per cent were sons and daughters of farmers, and 74 per cent of all the students came from the contributing counties, which now included the Kesteven Division of Lincolnshire.

The Second World War had a devastating effect on the college, with all courses being cancelled in September 1939. Special six-week courses were offered as part of the basic training for Land Army girls, and in January 1940 controlled Ministry of Agriculture courses were started.

In 1946 the National Agricultural Advisory Service was formed, which totally altered the way in which the Sutton Bonington campus was run. In April 1946 the property was transferred from the county councils to University College Nottingham. The short-course scheme and certificate courses were phased out, and only the National Diploma in Dairying was retained.

A gathering of students who attended a Kingston College course on cheese-making with particular reference to Stilton cheese. This photograph was possibly taken in the autumn of 1895, shortly after the college opened. Henry Morris is standing with his hand on a milk churn, and Gerard Veen is sitting on the second chair from the right. Mr Benson, Henry Morris's manager, is sitting on the fourth chair from the right and directly behind him stands Julia, who became Henry Morris's 'wife'. Henry Morris went on to be one of the most successful Stilton cheese-makers of all time.

Making Stilton cheese, *c.* 1915. Two students are posing with curd ladles while two others check the curd strainer bags lying in the 'leads'. Boards, 'bits' and hoops are stacked on the hastener in the background.

Students transfer curd into linen strainers spread out in the 'leads', *c.* 1915. In the background a student is preparing a mould.

Members of staff instructing students on how to prepare curd, for making into small 'sampler' Stilton cheeses, *c.* 1915. Various size moulds (hoops) are stacked on the hastener in the background.

Students stirring in the starter milk, adding rennet and breaking up the curd, on the Stilton cheese-making course, just after the First World War.

Ground floor plan of the Midland Dairy Institute, Kingston College, 1905.

John Thorpe Crosher, when a student at Sutton Bonington in the 1930s. John went on to run Tuxford & Tebbutt, becoming one of the industry's leading authorities on Stilton cheese production.

5

The Dairies

Until Thomas Nuttall opened the first dairy for producing Stilton cheese on factory lines in 1875, at Beeby near Leicester, all Stiltons had been produced in farmhouse dairies by farmers' wives and daughters from their herds' surplus milk. With the opening of Nuttall's factory, which employed thirty people and purchased milk from surrounding farms, the decline of the farmhouse dairy began. The last commercially run farmhouse dairy closed in 1935 at Somerby near Leicester, only a few miles east of Beeby. Stilton was still made in the extensive farmhouse dairy at the Model Farm, Ingarsby Lodge (built in about 1880) until 1961 by Mrs Doris Marion Wright. Doris produced nine Stiltons in one making when surplus milk was available during the summer months, contrary to the Milk Marketing Board's recommendations. This cheese was distributed privately, and was not available on the open market. With the Beeby dairy dominating the world of blue cream cheese production after only three years of opening, many other cheese-makers began to take notice. Not least of these was Henry Morris of Saxelbye, who established a chain of farmhouse factory dairies around Melton Mowbray and in the Vale of Belvoir. His dairies won many cups and trophies for fine blue-veined cream cheeses. Thomas Nuttall himself expanded his operation to Melton Mowbray, and his son John started making Stilton cheese in a factory at Hartington in Derbyshire. In August 2005 Quenby Hall began producing Stilton cheese once more.

Of the nineteenth-century dairies that produced cheese, Webster's, the dairy at Saxelbye, is the oldest factory still producing Stilton in its original building. However, all the seven dairies making Stilton cheese today have a long association with the locality where they are situated.

Stilton cheese is unique in that it can only be made from the milk of cows grazed on the right type of grass grown over a specific type of underlying subsoil. Experiments in the manufacture of Stilton cheese in other districts of England have taken place, but the cheese that was produced, even though it was labelled Stilton, did not have the unique flavour and texture that denote true Stilton. One such dairy started producing Stilton cheese at Yeovil, Somerset, during the 1930s. Owned by Aplin & Barrett, the manageress and main Stilton cheese-maker was Mary Jobson, who learnt the craft of Stilton cheese manufacture at Long Clawson Dairy. In 1850 James Meadows moved from Leicestershire to a farm on Exmoor, and from his cows he produced and excellent Stilton cheese. Eventually he took up sheep farming. Only the pastures of parts of Leicestershire, Nottinghamshire and Derbyshire can provide the grass, fodder, hay and silage suitable for the production of this unique cheese. A standard of Stilton cheese production, built up over centuries, is still being maintained by the Stilton Cheese Makers' Association, which was established under the chairmanship of Edward Wilford of Long Clawson Dairy Ltd in June 1936. The following pages contain photographs from the seven dairies that today uphold this tradition.

Quenby

Quenby Hall, 1790. This magnificent Jacobean house was built by George Ashby between 1615 and 1620. The large dairy building pre-dates the main hall, possibly being built in the sixteenth century, originally as a farm support barn, to hold cattle, fodder and farming implements. From a very early date it would have contained a dairy. The Ashbys were a self-supporting farming family, brewing their own ale and of course making cheese for their own consumption. In the last quarter of the seventeenth century cheese production increased because of park enclosures that enabled better control of the grazing of cows and higher milk production. Evidence of this early cattle enclosure still remains as the ha-ha that surrounds the hall. At this time, a drum-shaped cheese called Lady Beaumont's cheese was being made at Quenby, which gained a considerable reputation when offered for sale at local markets, such as Stamford. Lady Mary Beaumont was the daughter of Sir Erasmus de la Fontaine of Kirby Bellars. She married Thomas Beaumont of Cole Orton (1633–1702), and was related to the Ashbys, to whose dairy at Quenby she gave her recipe, which was used by cheese-maker Elizabeth Scarborough. Quenby cheeses were produced in large quantities at the end of the seventeenth and beginning of the eighteenth century, and had some impact on cheese sales in Leicester. The Quenby cheese was a pressed cheese coloured with marsh marigold flowers, the petals being boiled with alum to produce a yellow dye, which was added to the milk. The rennet was possibly produced from goose grass. The curd was crumbled, wrapped in linen and pressed with a 57 lb weight. Like all cheese produced on farms, no matter how it was made, blue mould would form beneath the crust of the cheese, given the right conditions while in store and sufficient time.

From about 1715 the Quenby estate began to deteriorate because the Ashby family concentrated their energies on other estates they owned. The farm buildings and the hall fell into disrepair, and it is fairly certain that no cheese was being made there by 1720. In this year Elizabeth Scarborough married one of the Orton family of Little Dalby and began making her Quenby cheese, which later developed into a recognizable Stilton cheese because of demand.

In 1759 Quenby Hall was sold by Warring Ashby to Shuckburgh Ashby. He restored the hall and outbuildings, raising a family and running a farming estate that improved the standard of living of the estate workers and the villagers of Hungarton. Stilton cheese was now an important cash commodity, generating considerable income for the producers. Shuckburgh Ashby undoubtedly fitted out the dairy. This building could be considered one of the earliest purpose-built farming/factory dairies producing the cheese that eventually developed into Stilton. Shuckburgh Ashby was in contact with Cooper Thornhill. As Coutts' east of England representative buying corn, Thornhill had dealings with the Ashby estates, scattered across the Midlands. With Frances and William Pawlett, they marketed Quenby's unique cheese. In August 2005 Quenby Dairy commenced production of a new Stilton cheese in a new dairy to the east of the hall, under the direction of Freddie de Lisle.

The dairy at Quenby Hall, viewed from the courtyard, revealing its sixteenth-century features.

'Cwene-burg', the *c.* 760 Anglo-Saxon Queen's Manor. A group of houses in the open countryside raised flocks of sheep in this area. Ewes' milk was made into an unpressed cream cheese by the early inhabitants during the summer months. After the Norman Conquest the hamlet was called Quenby and by 1377 it contained ten houses. By 1486 the Ashby family had demolished the houses and built themselves a farmhouse with a dairy. Here is the imposing dairy at Quenby Hall. The eighteenth-century slate troughs and the drainage system were still *in situ* in the dairy at this end of the building, until a modernization programme took place in the early 1970s.

John Lambert setting up the milk pasteurizer, August 2005.

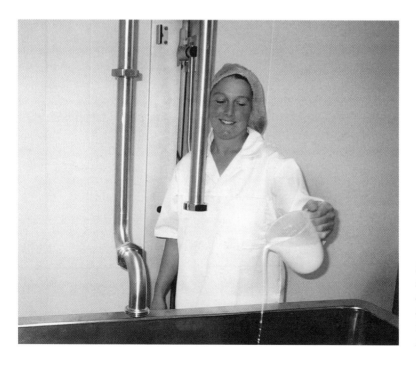

Sara Strong adding the starter into the cheese vat containing milk. The milk is obtained from cows grazing in fields near Quenby Hall, August 2005.

Sara Strong and John Lambert, Stilton cheesemakers. They are in front of the entrance to the sixteenth-century dairy at Quenby Hall. Sara is holding a Stilton cheese hoop and John is holding a Quenby Stilton, August 2005.

Webster's

Staff of the Saxelbye Dairy, *c.* 1930. On the front row to the right sits Edna, who married John Morris, Henry Morris's son. Henry founded the dairy in the early 1880s, and ran his business empire from this dairy until his death in 1920 (see p. 73). It then passed into the hands of the Webster family and was run very successfully by Mary and Julia Webster in 1924. It continued as Webster's Dairies through the Second World War. The Stockdale family ran the venture until it was purchased by the House of Callow in 1979.

Stilton **Cheese**

MEDALS
— AWARDED TO —
H. MORRIS,
Manor Farm, Saxelbye, Melton Mowbray.

FIVE CHAMPION CUPS, AND FORTY FIRST PRIZES AT LONDON DAIRY SHOWS, LEICESTERSHIRE AGRICULTURAL SHOWS, AND NUMEROUS OTHER PRIZES AT LOCAL SHOWS.

Winner of 7 First Prizes during 9 Years at the Royal Agricultural Society of England Shows previous to 1904.

FIRST PRIZE AT ROYAL SHOW FOR 1909, 1910, 1911, 1912.

Henry Morris's trade card, 1912. His dairies continued to win prizes after his death, and his main farmhouse dairy at Saxelbye still makes Stilton cheese. He set up this dairy in the early 1880s and was winning prizes at Islington Dairy Show by 1884, assisted by his wife Sarah, who died in 1909 aged 78.

Webster's Dairy, *c*. 1920. Curd draining in the leads. This process is no longer part of modern Stilton cheese production. The operation required skill and practice to avoid smashing the curd unnecessarily. The curd was ladled into one-yard squares of linen, the corners of which were drawn up and tied together. They were then allowed to settle in the troughs, where the whey drained away, as shown in this photograph. After three hours the parcels were turned and tightened, then allowed to drain for a further twelve hours. The curd was then tested for acidity before being broken up by hand and salt added. Next it was packed into the hoops, which can be seen stacked in the background of this photograph.

Margaret Knight cutting the curd, 1985.

Mark Frapwell displaying this dairy's speciality, organic Blue Stilton, November 1999.

Webster's Dairy, Saxelbye, has changed little in a hundred years. It is the smallest of the Stilton cheese producers, making about seventy-five cheeses per day. Milk is supplied by five farms in the village and surrounding area. One of the supplying farms is run by Richard Morris, the great grandson of Henry Morris. Richard works from the farmhouse (the Manor House) at which Henry started making Stilton cheese in the 1880s. Parts of the original dairy still survive.

Tuxford & Tebbutt

John Francis Crosher, who started making Stilton cheese in Tuxford & Nephews' warehouse at Thorpe End, Melton Mowbray, in 1909, under the direction of his father John Thorpe Crosher. In the very first year of production the dairy won the Swain Cup at the Leicestershire Agricultural Show (see p. 75). This firm had been factoring Stilton cheese from Melton Mowbray since the 1780s. In 1867 Messrs Tebbutt and Crosher, gentlemen's oufitters, decided to change their method of making a living by moving into the expanding pork pie business. Taking into the partnership William Thorpe Tuxford of Tuxford and Nephews, Stilton cheese factors, the two firms combined and shared the same premises. The pies were marketed under the name Tebbutt and Co., while the cheese was marketed under the name Tuxford and Nephews. From 1928 both manufacturing processes were marketed under one company name, Tuxford and Tebbutt Ltd. In 1966 they closed down the pork pie side of their business.

Tuxford and Tebbutt offices with their local sales shop in the background, left. Since the Second World War a number of changes of ownership have taken place. In 1940 the business was managed by John Francis Crosher and was taken over by John Thorpe Crosher, who was elected managing director in 1950. He sold the business to Express Foods in 1972, staying on as manager until 1978, when he handed over the operation to Mitch Farquarson. In September 1995 Express Foods sold the company to Waterford Dairies of Ireland, to be renamed Glanbia Foods, who then sold it on to Milk Link.

John Greenslade showing a party of schoolboys, on a job placement visit, how the recently installed milk pasteurizer works, 1947.

On 30 July 1958 the popular radio series 'Down Your Way' visited Melton Mowbray. One of the features was a tour of a Stilton cheese dairy. Here, at the loading bay at the dairy, are (left to right) Owen Cox, John Crosher, Franklin Engleman (holding a cheese iron) and a BBC programmer.

The extremely efficient Stilton cheese production area at Tuxford & Tebbutt, late 1980s. In the background are the vats where the milk is prepared, and in the middle ground are the draining tables where salt is added to the curd. The curd is then placed manually on to the conveyer system, where it is fed to a crumbling mill, mixed and placed in the hoops.

Wendy Berners and Trish Hughes rubbing up Stilton cheeses, 1988. In the background a hoop is being removed from a formed cheese.

Peter Wharton spreading salt on the curd in the draining tables, 1988.

Amanda Rudkin and a colleague packing quarter Stilton rings. This is a speciality of this dairy and is an excellent way of marketing the cheese.

Long Clawson

Long Clawson Dairy, 1932. On 6 November 1911 twelve farmers met in the village and formed a company to make Stilton cheese, under the chairmanship of Thomas Hoe Stevenson. The new company purchased the Royal Oak public house and on this site the dairy was built. The first manager was the skilled cheese-maker Tom Stockdale, to be followed by William McNair. This dairy has consistently made prize-winning Stilton cheeses, being awarded trophies in all the major dairy shows.

Churns stacked at the milk reception area, 1960. Until bulk transport methods were introduced, all milk was transported in churns. The success of this dairy lies in the fact that it is still a farmers' co-operative, obtaining top quality milk from its members. Consolidated in the 1930s, it was one of the leading forces behind the formation of the Stilton Cheese Makers' Association. During the Second World War only Cheddar cheese was made in the dairy. Tom Wiles was appointed chairman in 1945 and Stilton cheese production began again. Tom was awarded the MBE in 1974 and retired in 1976, being succeeded by his son John. Long Clawson Dairy had interests in the creameries at Harby and Hose, both producing Stilton.

A bulk delivery of milk, with Kim Kettle taking a sample for testing, 1975.

Filling a 1,000 gallon vat, 1975.

Peter Tinsley adding starter milk, half an hour before the rennet, 1975.

Peter Tinsley mixing in the starter milk and the rennet, 1975. This operation took five minutes, when milk was held in a 1,000 gallon vat.

Jean Morris cutting the curd, 1975. Undertaken one and a half hours after the rennet has been added, this releases the whey.

After most of the whey has been drained off, the curd is cut into blocks to allow further draining to take place, 1975.

Mrs Peggy Gunby turning young Stilton cheeses in the maturing room, 1975.

Curd milling, 1975. This breaks up the curd into walnut-sized pieces. Henrietta Widowson is bending down into the machine to check the quality.

Mrs Gillian Simon and Miss Pat Wright feeding the milling machine with blocks of curd, 1975. Stainless steel hoops are stacked to the right of the machine, waiting to be filled.

Mixing salt into the crumbled curd before it is packed into the moulds, 1975.

Stilton cheese is being removed from the moulds, rubbed up and then wrapped in linen binders, allowing it to sweat before being stacked in the maturing room. The wrapping of linen binders around Stilton cheese, as seen here in 1950, is no longer a part of the production process. Left to right: Miss Hilda Hallam, Mrs Sally Richardson, Mrs Hall.

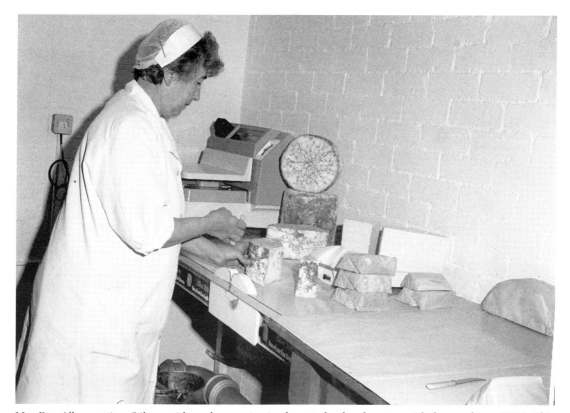

Mrs Peg Allen cutting Stilton with a cheese wire in the retail sales department before packing, 1975. This photograph shows off the superb marbling of a blue-veined Stilton cheese. There are a number of contributing factors that produce this blue mould, not least of all the presence of *Penicillium roqueforti* or *Penicillium glaucum*.

Full Stilton and half Stilton cheese, displayed with the 'Easom Bowl' by Neil Bailey, Chief Executive, and Peter Tinsley, selector of cheeses at the annual Melton and Belvoir Agricultural Society fat stock show and sale, when Long Clawson Dairy was awarded first prize and the coveted Easom Bowl, December 2000.

Colston Bassett

A milk wagon leaving Colston Bassett Dairy after delivering milk in seventeen gallon churns, 1923. Tom Coy, cheese-maker and manager from 1920 to 1960, is standing next to Charles Boyse at the rear of the lorry. This creamery was started in 1912 by sixteen local farmers and has consistently produced fine Stilton cheese ever since.

Curd being ladled into strainers, 1960. Left to right: Mrs M.E. Croft, Mrs F.M. Newton, Mrs C.M. Green.

Edith Stevens ladling curd into cooler trays, 1975.

In 1961 Colston Bassett Dairy won most of the major trophies for Stilton cheese production. Left to right: Melton Rose Bowl; Melton Fat Stock Show; Mathews & Skailes Challenge Cup, Olympia; the Leicestershire Agricultural Society's Challenge Cup; and the Best Stilton Cheese at the Oakham Show.

Ernie Wagstaff piercing Stiltons in the maturing room by machine, 1975. This was an improvement on the traditional method of using a hand-held steel needle (see p. 35). Ernie was appointed manager on the retirement of Tom Coy in 1960. Five farms now support the dairy, providing excellent milk from cows grazing in the Vale of Belvoir. This dairy is unique in that it has had only four managers since it was formed in 1912 by sixteen farmers with £16 share capital. The first manager was Eliza Wagstaff, a fine cheese-maker, followed by Tom Coy and now Richard Rowlett, who took over from Ernie Wagstaff in autumn 1996. It is still a small dairy, producing approximately ninety top quality Stilton cheeses per day.

Cropwell Bishop

Cropwell Bishop Creamery, makers of Stilton, Leicester, Cheshire, Derby and Cheddar cheeses, 1971. The history of the Cropwell Bishop Dairy is complex. No Stilton cheese was made at this village dairy until 1986. The parent company is Somerset Creameries Ltd, which started trading from Langport in Somerset. In 1947 Frank Strickland-Skailes expanded his Somerset cheese-making enterprises into Leicestershire, as he already owned the Cropwell Bishop Creamery. He purchased the dairy in North Street, Melton Mowbray, and obtained a 50 per cent holding in Waltham Dairy. Milk for both these dairies was pasteurized at Cropwell Bishop. In the early 1970s the operations in Somerset ceased, all cheese production being concentrated at Melton Mowbray and Cropwell Bishop.

Frank Strickland-Skailes, holding a trophy won at the London Dairy Show, 1960. In the background are photographs of Stilton cheese manufacture at his Melton Mowbray dairy, which closed down in 1986. All cheese made by Somerset Creameries Ltd is now made at Cropwell Bishop.

Bill Grennells sorting boxes of cheeses for distribution from the packing department at Cropwell Bishop, 1971: Melton Mowbray Farmers Coloured Cheddar, Devon Squire Cheddar, Melton Mowbray Dairy Farmer Caerphilly, and Golden Counties Melton Mowbray Stilton.

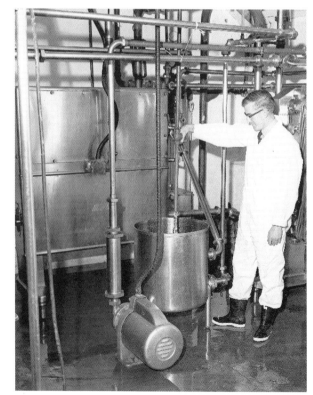

Andrew Caldwell pasteurizing milk at Cropwell Bishop in 1971 for use on site, and also for delivery to the North Street Dairy at Melton Mowbray.

Mabel Tyers, manageress at the North Street Dairy at Melton Mowbray, testing her Stiltons, 1970. Before working for Somerset Creameries Mabel ran the Stilton cheese-producing dairy at John-O-Gaunt.

Pauline Graves turning Stilton cheeses in the maturing room at Melton, 1984. The cheeses are wrapped in linen binders, and in the foreground (bottom right) is a stack of binders ready for washing. The operation of binding up young Stiltons with linen cloths has been discontinued in all the producing creameries.

First prize awarded to Somerset Creameries Ltd, Melton Mowbray Dairy Farmers for the best Stilton cheese at the Leicester Show, 1982.

At the 1997 Melton Mowbray Agricultural Show the coveted Easom Bowl for the best Stilton cheese was awarded to Cropwell Bishop Creamery. Left to right: Mario Addesso, cheesemaker; Ian Skailes, director; Linda Cregan, packaging manager; Andy Robinson, operations manager; and Howard Lucas, Stilton production manager.

Hartington

The picturesque village of Hartington nestling in an upper valley of the beautiful River Dove, *c.* 1905. Hartington Creamery is situated in the background to the left. A cheese-making dairy was opened on the site of the present dairy in 1876 by the Duke of Devonshire. It struggled as a business venture and closed in 1895. In 1900 Thomas Nuttall of Beeby purchased the building to commence making Stilton cheese. He first made Stilton cheese in Debyshire in the 1880s. By 1881 he was running a factory with his wife at Etwall and in 1883 he had expanded his Stilton cheese production to nearby Uttoxeter. He moved most of his business to this then-remote area to avoid the cattle plague (foot and mouth disease) and above all to obtain clean water from the River Dove. His son, John Marriott Nuttall, ran the business at Hartington.

John Nuttall (in white coat) standing outside his dairy, *c.* 1905. Joe Brindley is standing at the loading bay handling empty churns. When Nuttall's was formed into a limited company in 1916, Joe took over as manager because of the failing health of John Nuttall, whose wife Christina from then on effectively ran the business.

The staff of the Hartington cheese-making dairy just before the First World War. In the centre of the back row is John Nuttall, with his wife Christina sitting on a making-up pan on the front row. Joe Brindley is standing on the extreme left of the back row. In 1942 Joe Brindley purchased the business with his daughter Marjorie. After the Second World War, Joe set out to expand his Stilton cheese operation, purchasing dairies at Scalford, Wymeswold and Old Dalby.

J.M. Nuttall's, Hartington Creamery, *c.* 1960. In 1962 the business with all its remaining producing dairies was sold to the Milk Marketing Board, and became a division of Dairy Crest Foods in 1982.

A letterhead used in the 1920s and '30s.

BUCKINGHAM PALACE

1st March 1926.

Dear Sir,

I am desired by the Master of the Household to acknowledge the receipt of your letter of the 11th ult., and in reply to inform you that The King has been graciously pleased to approve of your being granted a Royal Warrant of Appointment as Purveyors of Cheese to His Majesty.

I enclose a letter containing the conditions of this grant, and I shall be much obliged if you will have the fly-leaf duly completed and returned to this office, in order that the Royal Warrant may be filled in correctly.

I am, Sir,
Yours faithfully,

Messrs. J.M. Nuttall and Co., Ltd.,
Dove Dairy,
Hartington,
Derbyshire.

The grant of a Royal Warrant.

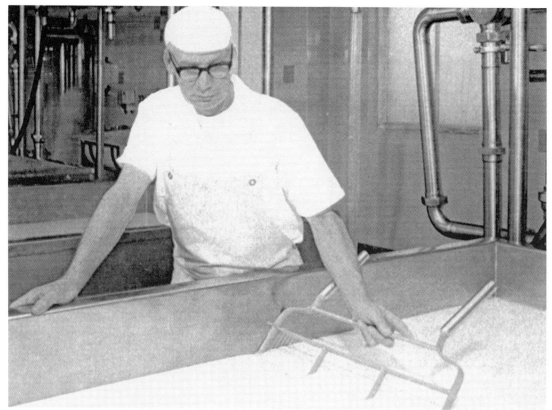

Percy Allcock cutting the curd, 1978.

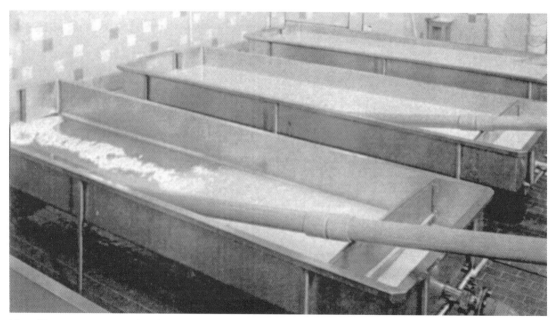

Nuttall's unique system of transferring the contents of the vats by pipes into coolers, which strain the whey from the curd, 1978.

Colin Dunn spreading salt over the curd, 1988.

Margaret Partridge and Elaine Millner smoothing the surface of young Stiltons with a flat knife.

Alan Salt testing Stiltons in Nuttall's extensive maturing room, 1978.

'Ye Olde Cheese Shoppe', Hartington, 1984. This picturesque shop stands off the village square in front of the duck pond. Run by J.M. Nuttall's, it sells the company's prize-winning cheeses to the public and the many tourists who visit the village during the summer months. As well as Stilton, other cheeses are on offer. One to be tried is Buxton Blue, developed at Hartington, which has a smooth texture, a warm russet colour and delicate blue veining.

Thomas Nuttall founded the very first factory producing Stilton cheese at the Manor house Dairy in the village of Beeby near Leicester. He also brewed beer in the village at the Beeby Brewery. Stilton cheese and fine beers have always complemented each other. In recognition of this fact, Nuttalls Dove Dairy at Hartington market their baby Stiltons in a very distinctive carton. On one side of the box this illustration commemorates the part that The Bell Inn at Stilton has played in the promotion of this famous blue veined cheese over the centuries down to the present day.

Nuttalls continue the tradition of producing prize-winning Stilton cheese that their founder first achieved in 1876. One hundred and twenty years later they were awarded the Easom Bowl for the best Stilton cheese exhibited at the Melton Mowbray Fat Stock Show, held on 10 December 1996.

GENUINE
Blue Stilton Cheese

The Bell Inn
Stilton, Huntingdonshire

The BBC chef Gary Rhodes being presented with a Hartington Creamery's half Stilton at a publishing promotion in Hammicks Bookshop, Peterborough, on the Dickinson and Morris stand, 13 December 1997. On the left is Stephen Hallam and on the right is Trevor Hickman, the author. The photograph was taken by Louise Waldron of Peterborough.

Brooksby

Brooksby Hall and Church, 1793. The hall had some interesting owners, not least the 7th Earl of Cardigan who led the charge of the Light Brigade at Balaclava, and later David Beatty who, as Vice Admiral, was in charge of the British Fleet at the Battle of Jutland. In 1945 the hall was purchased by Leicestershire County Council and developed into the famous agricultural college. In the year 2000 after a merger it became Brooksby Melton College.

A promotion of the world-famous Stilton cheese at Brooksby Agricultural College: a cross section of members of the public as Stilton cheese tasters, 1998. Left to right: Sharon Grech, lecturer from Southfields College School of Catering; Pam Hickman, housewife; Trevor Hickman, author of *The History of Stilton Cheese*; Andrea Smith, Consumer Affairs Analyst for the *Leicester Mercury*; Edwina Baker-Courtenay, Hotel Services Manager, Brooksby College; Kevin Stanley, Head Chef, Brooksby College.

6

A Gourmet Delight

'Stilton is for everyone.' The Romans enjoyed a strong-tasting, blue-veined cream cheese, and must have found this type of cheese being produced when they invaded England. It has been popular ever since. The author of this book has attempted to place this unique cheese in its correct place in English history. Today Stilton cheese is as popular as it has ever been, enjoyed by millions of people around the world. Stilton can be eaten with a glass of wine, port or beer, or as individual tastes dictate. In the following pages are four recipes showing how Stilton cheese can complement and enhance other dishes. There are hundreds of ways in which this cheese can be incorporated into interesting recipes, to delight the palates of gourmets everywhere.

Presentation of food is everything, and is today as important as it has ever been. Stilton served in a fine Stilton bell is magnificent. In large family gatherings for lunch and dinner in the villages around Melton Mowbray, it was, and still is, served in this way on some tables, after the sweet course has been served. The ritual is that the host introduces the port to the left and Stilton to the right, traditionally to be served with a silver scoop (see p. 65). Today it is considered wiser to use a Stilton server, allowing the cheese to be cut level in neat wedges, avoiding waste and enabling the cheese to be stored correctly between servings.

Cheese has always been available in public houses and inns where food is offered, and no self-respecting English restaurant, public house or hotel should be without Stilton. The King of Cheese, the cheese of middle England, should take pride of place along with all the other fine English cheeses. The author has located two public houses that are named after this famous cheese, all serving fine Stilton. All the producing dairies make excellent Stilton cheese to a basic formula but to their own individual recipes. Mature Stiltons of a similar age presented from all six dairies will have slightly different flavours, and preference for cheese from individual dairies can develop. What is important is how the maturing cheese is stored and retailed. Stilton at its best is a moist cheese: it must never be allowed to become dry. Speciality shops and 'educated' retailers are aware of this, although unfortunately some wholesale outlets are not.

Stilton cheese, when Cooper Thornhill began factoring it, was very much a seasonal trade and in some quarters it is still considered a cheese for Christmas. It should not be viewed that way; rather it is a cheese for all seasons, to be eaten by all, 'full of energy'. Captain Scott, on his first journey to the Antarctic, was given six Stilton cheeses by Henry Morris from his Saxelbye Dairy. He returned to tell the tale. On his last fateful journey to the South Pole, Scott did not take any Stilton with him. Would history have been different if he had been eating Stilton cheese, thus building up his team's stamina?!

John and Norma Major being presented with the first Stilton Bell cheese dish by designer Richard Landy (right) and the owner of the Bell Inn, Liam McGivern, 1996.

Joan and Robert Watson receiving a cheque for promoting cheese sales, 1984. Joan and Robert ran a speciality cheese shop in Bingham from 1977 to 1986, stocking only the best types of cheese. They held in store more than a hundred varieties. Most of the cheeses were stored at the Old Dairy at Harby until Robert determined that they were mature enough to sell. Farmhouse Cheddar was held for six months before being retailed. Their speciality Stilton was made at Colston Bassett Dairy.

Stilton Stands

Ann Walker offering a cut of half a Stilton cheese, produced by Long Clawson Dairy. The Melton Cheeseboard is situated in Bowley Court on Windsor Street, Melton Mowbray. It is an excellent shop in which to purchase prize-winning Stilton cheese and Wedgwood Stilton stands.

George Jones' 'Apple Blossom' majolica Stilton cheese stand, *c.* 1880. (For further reading on Stilton cheese stands, please consult Audrey Dudson's *Cheese Dishes*, 1993.)

Unattributed grey Staffordshire Stilton cheese stand, *c.* 1880.

Light blue Wedgwood Stilton cheese stand, *c.* 1850.

Blue and white Spode Stilton cheese stand, *c.* 1820.

Recipes

Stilton and Leek Soup (serves 4).

1 oz butter, 1 onion, chopped, 6 oz leeks, sliced, 1 oz flour, ¾ pint fresh milk, 4 oz Blue Stilton cheese, crumbled, freshly ground pepper, 3 oz natural yoghurt.

Melt the butter in a saucepan. Add onion and leeks, and fry for 5 minutes until soft. Stir in flour and stock, then heat, whisking, until soup thickens, to blend in the boiling stock. Add bouquet garni and simmer over a low heat for 20 minutes. Cool slightly, remove bouquet garni and liquidize soup. Return to pan or dish. Add milk and heat until almost boiling. Remove from heat. Add cheese, pepper and yoghurt, and stir until cheese has melted. Serve hot.

Blue Stilton Soufflé

(serves 8 as a starter).

1 pint double cream, 6 oz Blue Stilton cheese, crumbled, 6 eggs, pinch of grated nutmeg, 1 small clove of crushed garlic, salt, cayenne pepper to taste.

Liquidize eggs, cheese, nutmeg, garlic, salt and pepper together until smooth. Add cream and liquidize again. Pour into eight well-buttered ramekins and sprinkle with nutmeg. Bake at 375°F, gas mark 5, for 30 minutes until browned and set. Serve immediately.

Stilton and Banana Bake
(serves 4 as a starter).
4 bananas, 4 slices lean roast ham, English mustard, ¾ pint white sauce, 4 oz Blue Stilton cheese, crumbled.
Peel the bananas, spread each slice of ham with a little English mustard and wrap round each banana. Secure with a wooden cocktail stick. Place in a large ovenproof dish, pour over white sauce, sprinkle with Stilton cheese and bake at 350°F, gas mark 4, for about 25 minutes or until golden and bubbling.

Steak and Stilton (serves 4).
4 sirloin steaks, trimmed of fat, each weighing about 8 oz, 4 oz Blue Stilton cheese, crumbled, 1 oz butter, softened.
Mash the crumbled Stilton in a bowl with a fork. Add the butter and mix in. Season to taste. Put the steaks on the grill rack and season with plenty of pepper. Put under a preheated grill and cook for 2–10 minutes on each side, according to preference. Remove the steaks from the grill, spoon the Stilton mix evenly over them. Grill for one further minute. Serve hot, accompanied with boiled new potatoes and mixed salad, or vegetables of your choice.

Alternatively, select four 8 oz fillet steaks, cut to a drum shape and grill to taste. Remove from grill and with a sharp knife make two horizontal cuts evenly spaced. Place a slice of Stilton cheese in each cut. Grill for a further minute, allowing the cheese to melt.

Public Houses

The Stilton Cheese Inn, Chapel Lane, Somerby, near Melton Mowbray. The village of Somerby gained a reputation as a centre for Stilton cheese between the First and Second World Wars because of the excellent cheese that was made by Frank Fryer at Manor Farm (see pp. 86–8). Stilton cheese can be enjoyed at this fine public house, incorporated into a variety of dishes on an interesting menu in the charming restaurant.

The Stilton Cheese, Stilton, formerly The George (see p. 48). Stilton cheese can be purchased to take away as well as being enjoyed in the restaurant at this traditional public house. This inn was named The Stilton Cheese in 1926.

'Wedge of Stilton'

To celebrate the 300th anniversary of the birth of Cooper Thornhill (1705–59), Richard Landy, a potter living in Stilton, has produced this cheese dish.

It was largely due to the efforts of Cooper Thornhill, legendary 18th century landlord of the Bell Inn, Stilton, and his business partner Frances Pawlett, cheesemaker of Wymondham in Leicestershire, that the cheese we know today as Stilton became established as a quality product that is universally recognized, respected and protected.

THIS BOX CONTAINS AN AUTHENTIC

'Wedge of Stilton'

CHEESE DISH

Handcrafted in Stilton by Richard Landy

The label from a package containing a 'Wedge of Stilton', a cheese dish produced in Stilton, Cambridgeshire.

Packaging

Stilton cheese can only be made in the counties of Leicestershire, Nottinghamshire and Derbyshire, as they contain the correct type of pasture for grazing cows to provide the milk necessary for this unique cheese. It is the only British cheese protected by a certification trade mark. To avoid misunderstandings with regard to the high standards expected by customers, the Stilton Cheese Makers' Association, through legislation, maintains strict controls on the producers. Even so, problems still occur. Between 1970 and 1974 considerable correspondence and newspaper comment took place concerning the use of the word Stilton by an American cheese manufacturer. The chairman of the Stilton Cheese Makers' Association at that time was Robert Watson, who led the fight supported by the Lord Lieutenant of Leicestershire, Colonel Andrew Martin, together with Miss Mervyn Pike MP and the Right Honourable Geoffrey Howe MP for the Department of Trade and Industry. The campaign to have the name Stilton removed from the packaging used to promote the blue-veined cheese made in Wisconsin was finally successful, aided by lawyers from Graham Campaign & McCarthy of New York who acted for the Stilton Cheese Makers' Association. This photograph is of one of the cartons that held the 'American Stilton'. How it compared with the genuine cheese is anybody's guess.

Baskets

Wicker baskets were specially made to hold full and half Stiltons. They were never uniform in size because different dairies produced different sized Stiltons. Developed to hold Stilton cheese during the stage coach era, they became very popular for transporting individual cheeses by rail. The cheese was well tied down with twine and securely labelled (see p. 59).

Acknowledgements

The author has taken many years compiling information for this book, and he is indebted to many people. Two of them deserve special mention, because without their researches the book could never have been written. Thanks must go to Ralph Peniston Taylor, who translated the documents written in Norman French (part of the Harleian collection in the British Museum), which enabled the author to unravel the early history of Stilton cheese production. He also collated it in order and detailed the involvement of the Hamelins, the Berkeleys and the Pawletts. Squire de Lisle of Quenby Hall has diligently collected large amounts of information concerning the history and production of Stilton cheese, and made all his personal collection available to the author. This material was invaluable. The author also records his thanks to the following people, who have provided both information and historic photographs:

Neil Bailey of Long Clawson Dairy • Andy Wiles • Jean Morris • Nigel White, secretary of the Stilton Cheese Makers' Association • Alan Oliver • John Crosher • Joan Watson • Francis Fryer • Mrs P. Anderson • Rigby Graham • Bill Hewson • Stan Cramer and the University of Nottingham • Philip Saunders and Lesley James of the County Record Office, Huntingdon • Len Hewitt • Cherry Bishop • Robert Fairbrother • Keith Davis • Harold Fox of the Department of English Local History, Leicester University • Christine Mason of the Bodleian Library • Gill Musson • Peter Hubbard • John Lambert of Scalford Dairy • Sarah Tomlinson • Liam McGivern of the Bell Inn, Stilton • The staff of the Leicestershire Record Office • Olive Middleton of Osborne Publicity Services, Buxton • Helen Callow of Webster's Dairy • Mitch Farquharson of Tuxford & Tebbutt • Richard Davies of Millway Foods, Harby • Steve Peace and Alan Salt of J.M. Nuttall, Hartington • Miss J. Brindley • David and Ian Skailes of Cropwell Bishop Dairy • Ernie Wagstaff and Richard Rowlett of Colston Bassett Dairy • Alan Wright • Richard Landy • Dorothy Lovett • Jeanette Finch • Joe Ecob

Thanks must also be recorded to the many people in the villages the author visited on his travels who have provided snippets of information, and a special thank you to the staff of all the dairies that the author visited during autumn 1994 and spring 1995: their advice and help was invaluable. Thanks go out to the author's wife and family who have lived with Stilton cheese for very many months – although this may not have proved too much of a hardship when it was served on the author's table. Angela Edwards spent long hours sorting out the author's manuscript, enabling a draft to be presented to the publishers, for which grateful thanks are recorded. Finally, most of the photographs printed here are covered by copyright and permission has been granted to reproduce them. However, should this not be the case concerning some photographs, Trevor Hickman offers his sincere apologies for reproducing them without permission and will make an acknowledgement in future editions.

LIST OF PLACES AND FEATURES